Jean Baudrillard

Modern European Thinkers
Series Editor: Professor Keith Reader,
University of Newcastle upon Tyne

The Modern European Thinkers series offers low-priced introductions for students and other readers to the ideas and work of key cultural and political thinkers of the postwar era.

also available

Edgar Morin
Myron Kofman

Pierre Bourdieu
Jeremy F. Lane

Walter Benjamin
Esther Leslie

André Gorz
Conrad Lodziak and *Jeremy Tatman*

Gilles Deleuze
John Marks

Guy Hocquenghem
Bill Marshall

Georges Bataille
Benjamin Noys

Régis Debray
Keith Reader

Julia Kristeva
Anne-Marie Smith

Jean Baudrillard

In Radical Uncertainty

Mike Gane

Pluto Press

LONDON • STERLING, VIRGINIA

First published 2000 by Pluto Press
345 Archway Road, London N6 5AA
and 22883 Quicksilver Drive, Sterling, VA 20166-2012, USA

www.plutobooks.com

British Library Cataloguing in Publication Data
A catalogue record for this book is available from the British Library

ISBN   0 7453 1636 0 hardback
ISBN   0 7453 1635 2 paperback

Library of Congress Cataloging in Publication Data

Gane, Mike.
    Jean Baudrillard: in radical uncertainty / Mike Gane.
       p.   cm. – (Modern European thinkers)
    Includes bibliographical references.
    ISBN 0–7453–1636–0 (hbk)
       1. Baudrillard, Jean. 2. Sociology—France—Philosophy.
    3. Sociology—France—History—20th century. I. Title. II. Series.
    HM479.B38 G36 2000
    301′.01—dc21   00-026011

Designed and produced for Pluto Press by
Chase Production Services
Typeset from disk by Marina Typesetting, Minsk, Belarus
Printed in the European Union by T J International, Padstow

Contents

Abbreviations

Abbreviations used in the text for major works by Jean Baudrillard

A	*America*
BL	*Baudrillard Live*
CM	*Cool Memories*
CMII	*Cool Memories II*
CS	*The Consumer Society*
EC	*The Ecstasy of Communication*
EDI	*The Evil Demon of Images*
EI	*L'Échange impossible*
ET	*Écran total*
FCM	*Fragments: Cool Memories III*
FCPES	*For a Critique of the Political Economy of the Sign*
FF	*Forget Foucault*
FS	*Fatal Strategies*
GD	*La Gauche divine*
GWNP	*The Gulf War Did Not Take Place*
IE	*The Illusion of the End*
ISSM	*In the Shadow of the Silent Majorities*
LBEW	*Looking Back at the End of the World*
MP	*The Mirror of Production*
P	*Paroxysm*
PC	*The Perfect Crime*
PFM	*Please Follow Me*
S	*Seduction*
SED	*Symbolic Exchange and Death*
SO	*The System of Objects*
SS	*Simulacra and Simulation*
TE	*The Transparency of Evil*

Preface

Jean Baudrillard remains highly controversial, a lone individual thinker without a school or an attachment to a social movement or intellectual discipline. He is often read simply as a leading French intellectual. In 1997 he was one of those criticised by Alan Sokal and Jean Bricmont *Intellectual Impostures* (Sokal & Bricmont 1998), when suddenly many people who had not read a word of the French philosophers attacked (Lacan, Kristeva, Irigaray, Latour, Deleuze, Lyotard, Virilio and Baudrillard) became highly knowledgeable about these authors. I restrict discussion of Sokal and Bricmont to an examination of their short critique of Baudrillard's use of scientific terminology in the chapter on uncertainty (Chapter 5). But it is interesting to note that one of Baudrillard's own themes is that of simulacra and simulation, and indeed he writes of science as a vast simulation model. The question addressed in this book is not therefore the same as that of Sokal and Bricmont, which asked whether Baudrillard has an adequate basis to talk about nuclear physics or advanced mathematical theories.

It is certainly true that Baudrillard has shown increasing interest in developments in science, in mathematics, astronomy, chemistry, biology and in physics in particular, as well as the technologies associated with them. He evidently regards some of them as forms of what he has called 'radical theory'. He has tried to define and advocate this form of theorising in his latest writings as appropriate to the situation where the radicality of the world far outstrips that of its concept in cultural theory. It is perhaps at this point that the central but hidden thesis of Sokal and Bricmont should be made clear: they argue that the whole idea of a radical break in the sciences, a revolutionary passage from modern to postmodern science as argued by Lyotard, is largely pure fiction, a serious misunderstanding, a serious philosophical error. The so-called war on the abuse of science by certain philosophers – 'C'est la guerre' said *Le Figaro* – had something in common with Baudrillard's own notion of the displacement of objectives in modern 'war' (see Chapter 8). Baudrillard is one thinker, among many, who not only goes along with the idea that there are a number of basic revolutions within the sciences, but also seeks out important consequences of these revolutions for cultural analysis. What is at issue is whether and to what extent there is a shift, and how to think about its consequences. Sokal himself is content to say 'I'm an unabashed

Old Leftist who never quite understood how deconstruction was supposed to help the working class ... a stodgy old scientist who believes, naively, that there exists an external world' (Sokal & Bricmont 1998: 249).

To read Baudrillard is to follow a particular line of analysis which not only accepts the shift in the sciences but also registers it as one aspect of a process that affects every element in society and culture. Readers who immediately supported the theses developed by Sokal and Bricmont seemed to accept that this was indeed the issue: the world has not changed fundamentally, there is no need to think or act differently in today's world, for time and space, cause and effect, true and false, right and wrong, subject and object, are what they always were and are related as they have always been. But though people live as they always have, in the sense that they breathe, walk and converse, Baudrillard's thesis that the world is changing more radically than thought itself corresponds at least to wide experience and that is why his imaginative responses have a significant readership.

This book argues that commentators on Baudrillard's work have themselves not kept pace with changes in his writing and theory. It presents an introductory critical overview of his basic ideas in the first three chapters, and then begins to examine the evolution of his more recent ideas. Throughout this discussion attention is given to an assessment of what Baudrillard's recent writing tries to achieve, and whether he comes near to achieving it, particularly in his analyses of reality and hyperreality (Chapter 4), of the technological revolution (Chapter 6), of transformed relations of sex and gender (Chapter 7), of violence and war (Chapter 8) and of art and photography (Chapter 9).

I would like to thank a number of people for special inspiration, assistance and advice with this book: Chris Rojek, Chris Turner, Nicholas Zurbrugg, William Pawlett, William Merrin, John Marks, Mariam Fraser, Marcus Doel, Richard Smith, Keith Ansell-Pearson, Andrew Wernick, Nicholas Gane and Monique Arnaud. I have presented papers on Baudrillard's work and benefited from subsequent discussions at the Universities of Essex, Lancaster, Nottingham, De Montfort at Leicester, Warwick and Oxford. Many thanks to all those, particularly to colleagues and students at Loughborough University, who have discussed and argued over the issues covered in this book. I have drawn on and in some cases updated essays published in *Modern and Contemporary France* (no. 44), *Theory Culture and Society* (1995 vol. 12 no. 4; and 1999 vol. 16 no. 5–6), *Parallax* (1999 vol. 5 no. 1), and in *A Companion to Continental Philosophy* (Critchley & Schroeder 1998). Part of the chapter on art was presented at an international conference on 'Baudrillard and Art' in Grenoble and published in *Sans Oublier Baudrillard* (Majastre 1996). The chapter on technology was presented at an International Conference at the University of Northumbria at Newcastle in 1999 and published in *Angelaki* (1999

vol. 4 no. 2). Part of the concluding chapter was presented at an
International Conference in Cork, Ireland in 1999. Part of the chapter
on reality was presented at an International Conference at Brunel
University in 1999.

At this point the author is rightly obligated to acknowledge that
the inevitable errors in the work are his own responsibility. But this
opens on to one of the 'paradoxes of the preface' (Poundstone 1991:
135). If there is an error, but it is not precisely identified, any particular
statement might be that error, so no particular statement can be
accepted with any complete certainty. Perhaps, though, the error in
the book is precisely this error and there are no subsequent ones. Even
then the preface is correct. There is another paradox of interest and
relevance mentioned by Derrida. Any preface is a contradiction because
it states what is about to be stated again: otiose, or a strange doubling
– 'preceding what ought to be able to present itself on its own, the
preface falls like an empty husk, a piece of formal refuse' (Derrida
1981: 9). Perhaps the preface contains a secret. If it sums up the work
to come it is therefore 'the simulacrum of a postface ... while pretending
to turn around to look backwards, one is also starting over again,
adding extra text ... opening up within the labyrinth a supplementary
digression, which is also a false mirror that pushes the labyrinth's
infinity back forever ... '(Derrida 1981: 27).

But Baudrillard does not work to an idea of infinity ('a concept
which corrupts all others' (Borges 1970: 237)) or of the labyrinth.
He does not work to that of chance, the aleatoric, in any simple sense
either. Thus in his book *L'Échange impossible* (Baudrillard 1999: 79–
88) he considers one of the classic fictional investigations of this theme,
Luke Rhinehart's *The Dice Man* (Rhinehart 1994). The Dice Man is
a psychologist who begins to let his dilemmas and options be decided
by throwing dice, and who elaborates this into a theology of chance:
'In the beginning was Chance ... and he dwelt among us, full of chaos,
and falsehood and whim' (Ibid. 6). An epigraph of Rhinehart's text is
taken from Chuang-Tze, and is often cited by Baudrillard: 'The torch
of chaos and doubt – that is what the sage steers by.' Another epigraph
is from Nietzsche: 'I am Zarathustra the godless: I cook every chance
in my pot' (Ibid. 9). Baudrillard rejects Rhinehart's view of all this
and is clearly not a Dice Man himself.

The difference is highly instructive and perhaps informs also about
other issues such as his rejection of postmodernism. His critique points
to logical and ideological difficulties in the Dice Man's project. First
of all the Dice Man's project is itself not determined by the throw of
the dice; second, the six outcomes are convenient options ('never
include an option I might be unwilling to fulfill' (Ibid. 89)). As the
initial decision binds the Dice Man to his obligations, it is clear that
in attempting to pass into the liberty promised by escaping the
constraint to make his own decisions, he has only landed himself in a

higher servitude. According to Baudrillard, Rhinehart thinks, falsely, that chance is instituted by the throw of the dice. In fact the higher order of chance and destiny lies in brute existence itself, in the immanent disorder of the world. Rhinehart logically moves to become an agent of evil itself, but all such ideas (and he mentions de Sade, and *Liaisons Dangereuses*) fail to arrive at a genuinely *fatal* order because such attempts at the deregulation of the world are programmed in advance. Not only that, but in today's world such programmes and their outcomes do not seem in any way to alter the shape of things (the sphere of speculation does not seem to impinge on the 'real' world: whether God exists or not changes nothing (EI: 84)). Rhinehart's rule of chance is redundant. The idea that the rule of the dice releases the 'I' into a plurality of possible destinies Baudrillard describes as naive 'superstition', for Destiny – and here Baudrillard leans on one of the cornerstones of his position – arises only within a dual relation, 'never one that is multiple or plural' (EI: 86). Thus in the end the novel moves to a characterisation of 'deregulation in *trompe l'oeil*' – Dice Therapy, Dice Centres, the logic of cults and power.

In this book on Baudrillard's work I try to identify critiques such as this as indications of an attempt to chart a course, to work out a strategy; this inevitably involves drawing lines, making judgements, and taking a position which argues that in order to grasp the world, chance and uncertainty have to be defined in the most radical way, and all the consequences of this radicality have to be registered in the analysis of things.

CHAPTER 1

Jean Baudrillard

Who are you then, J.B., you who speak of
simulacra, but a simulacrum yourself? (FCM: 22)

Jean Baudrillard was born in Reims in the Ardennes region of north-
eastern France in July 1929. As he has himself pointed out, he was
born under the sign of the Lion, just after Black Thursday in the year
of the great crash. He came from a family which had moved into the
city and had become part of the *petit fonctionnariat*, and who still had
strong roots in the peasant culture of the countryside. He was a brilliant
pupil but his academic career was highly unusual. Preparing for the
école normale supérieure, he abandoned his studies after three months
in the *hypokhagne* and 'ran away'. He nevertheless eventually qualified
as a language teacher and spent a decade teaching in provincial *lycées*.
In the 1960s he made the transition to sociology under the guidance
of Henri Lefebvre and Roland Barthes by an 'indirect route', taking
up a position teaching sociology at Nanterre in October 1966. He
stayed in the university for 20 years. It was, it seems, for the latter
part not a happy experience. He was offered a position in the United
States but turned it down (P: 80). He successfully presented his doctorate
in early 1986 at the Sorbonne and retired from university teaching in
1987 in order to write (since then he has published over ten books),
to take up lecturing engagements all over the world, and to indulge
his passion: photography (books of photographs were published in
1989 and 1999 following a number of successful exhibitions).

Encounters

Something of the man can be gleaned from the accounts of those who
have beaten a path to his door for an interview. For example, a report
in the magazine *The Face* for 1989, noted that in person, 'Baudrillard
doesn't quite look the part. From his books you expect maybe a witty,
seductive rake. He actually looks a little like a union boss. He's
thickset, wears mostly brown, and rolls his own.'[1] In 1994 Peter
Hamilton wrote:

> To reach his place you must first locate the entrance in a nondescript
> street, then punch in a code to gain entry to the building, and mount
> the interminable staircase that leads to his fifth-floor apartment

...The door swings open to reveal an elegantly casual, smiling Jean Baudrillard. And inside all is white walls, a durrie thrown over the settee, a kilim on the floor ... It is a surprise to learn that Baudrillard only acquired a television in 1981.[2]

Then in 1996, Chris Horrocks, the author of *Baudrillard for Beginners*, also went to Paris:

Balding, bespectacled, and soberly dressed, Baudrillard is seated at the sturdy table in the living room ... it's bright and comfortable, and, well, normal. There is is even a large modern TV and sound system ...White walls bear the framed outpourings of Baudrillard's sideline of photography ... Beyond is the room where he taps out his wisdom on an old electric typewriter ...The unrepentant loner puffs a cigarette as we mull over the problem of the millennium and whether it will happen. His brand of tobacco is *Caporal* and he rolls his own with a little machine.[3]

In 1997 Michael Fordham also took the trip to Montparnasse for an interview which appeared in *Dazed and Confused*: 'A genial disposition and the playfully ambiguous nature of his discourse betray an intellectual bob and weave ... Conversing with Baudrillard makes you giddy. His ideas spin over and untangle themselves as they are uttered.'[4] And in 1998, William Leith made the pilgrimage for the *Observer*:

When I reach his building, I have no idea how to get in. I do not know the coded number to dial into the wall ... [Eventually ...] I punch the number into the keypad ... I open the door and walk into a broad hall ... the door closes behind me. Then, weirdly, the light snaps off; I am in total darkness. I cannot see ahead of me ... Somewhere along the wall, at shoulder height I find the light. There is a lift, but I take the steep stairs.

I ring the bell ... The door opens. A smallish, compact man, definitely the eyebrow-raiser from the photographs, opens the door and backs away. He is wearing an expensive, open-necked shirt and a V-neck sweater of very fine wool ... He smiles gently. He looks at his watch. I am, of course, late. Time is short.

The appartment is bathed in light, and uncluttered. The carpet is light brown, the walls white. There is a desk and a bentwood chair. There is a wafer-thin television set ...

The parting is quite formal. He shakes my hand with his small neat one ... This time I take the lift. I was not disappointed; Baudrillard was not deadly serious, and he was not a joker. He was disengaged calm, witty.[5]

It is remarkable how observant his visitors are.

Baudrillard's journals

But Baudrillard is encountered elsewhere. Richard Gott, in 1994, had a dinner appointment with him, and wrote:

> I slipped out on Friday to have lunch with Jean Baudrillard, the most significant thinker of the age. He had oysters, I had *potage du jour* ... one particular sentence might help intransigent disbelievers to understand why he has such a cult following. Life-style and values, he argues, rather than economic need, form the basis of social life ... [6]

Baudrillard's journal noted that he had met Richard Gott in London: 'Eating tepid oysters and caviar with a KGB mole in a London restaurant.'[7]

Baudrillard's journals note that he had been in London for the launching of the English translation of one of his books, *Symbolic Exchange and Death*. He had given talks at the French Institute, the ICA, given interviews, been shopping, met his publishers, met his English translator. None of this appears in his journal. In fact he wrote:

> I have had an attack of renal colic (stomach pains). Now, I remember my last attack was fifteen years ago and that it occurred in Tubingen, where I had gone for the presentation of the German translation of *Symbolic Exchange and Death* ... (FCM: 127)

Then the journal breaks into abstract theoretical reflections on exchange. And one of the curious things is that Baudrillard had encountered an English audience engaged in reading his book on the gift and symbolic exchange, and yet he wrote in his journal: 'The gift, for its part, is not only possible but ... *fatal*. It is the very form of impossible exchange' (FCM: 127).

Baudrillard seems used to handling this kind of systematic disjunction between two orders: the order of his interlocutors or readers and his own. It seems clear that in some respects Baudrillard remains outside the communication. The position he likes to occupy is one step out of synchrony. Because he is not where you believe he is, there is always a sort of vertigo in the encounter, and thus always something of the unexpected in reading him. For example, in the pages which follow his notes on his visit to London, there is a brief comment which appears to have been written immediately after the death of his mother:

> ... a sudden void which will have to be filled by a secret amassing of guilt. For successful mourning is always the equivalent of a virtual murder ... And it is not just the living who perform their work of mourning; the dead must also do so. They have to give up the living to be really dead ... (FCM: 132)

So behind the journals there is a 'real' life. The jottings are fragments which set the abstract and the concrete side by side. But what kind of things do we find out from the journals? Evidently quite a lot, since we even know what Baudrillard thinks about the stairs to his apartment: 'I have long wondered why my five flights of stairs are mysteriously more difficult to climb than other people's.' He reflects, 'There can be no doubt that they would be less difficult if I didn't live there, if I did not expect to find my double, whom I would really like to lose, at the top of them' (FCM: 17).

The journals in fact start with entries in 1980 with *Cool Memories* 1980–85, and include so far *Cool Memories* II, *Fragments: Cool Memories* III (1990–95), and *America*. We follow not only Baudrillard's travels, for example to Latin America, North America, Australia, Europe, Japan and India, but also his personal relations and his encounters. But all of these encounters are rendered quasi-fictional since no sense of completeness of contextualisation is offered.

At least one quasi-fictional riposte has been written against Baudrillard. Sylvère Lotringer published a long interview with Baudrillard called *Forget Baudrillard*, and edited the Foreign Agents series which introduced important Baudrillard texts to the English-speaking world. But at a conference devoted to Baudrillard's ideas held in Montana in 1989 (Stearns & Chaloupka 1992: 1) just after the publication of *America*, Lotringer presented a paper called 'Hyperreal' (Stearns & Chaloupka 1992: 38–42) which was an apparently fictionalised portrait of Jean Baudrillard encountering someone called Marshall Blonsky. Baudrillard is a 'stocky man with a plain face and thick, dark rimmed glasses' who drives a Cherokee Jeep and transports Blonsky through the snow to his log cabin in the Adirondack hills. Blonsky is shocked to find that the cabin had only one room with no computer: 'the hyper-modern man *wrote by hand*' and drank herbal tea and kept a golden retriever and a cat. Baudrillard begins to talk: 'Since the breaking up of my marriage I had new insights into myself ... here in my cabin, I'm safe. I can make whatever sounds that come out of me. I can come back here and just be. And that's precious. I moved back here, so to speak, in 1980 ... ' Finally Baudrillard says, 'I believe I know who I am' and Blonsky asks, 'And who are you, Monsieur Baudrillard?' 'Don't you see?' comes Baudrillard's reply: 'I'm a rebel.'

There does not appear to be a record of Baudrillard's thoughts on the conference or on this paper by Lotringer. But clearly what Lotringer presents as astounding is the sheer contrast between Baudrillard and the image that must be projected of the traveller in hyperreality known as 'Jean Baudrillard'. Indeed it is this discrepancy which is 'hyperreal'.[8] Baudrillard makes no secret of the fact that he does not use a computer, but writes by hand and uses an electric typewriter (CM: 81).[9] He is also, as noted, keen on photography, and his recently published book of photographs indeed has two pictures of his writing table (one of

1986, and another of 1996). The later photograph shows an open notebook with a pen on it with another single page with handwriting and a typewritten manuscript. By the side there is a glass ashtray. The hyper-modern man writes by hand and then takes a photograph of his manuscript – a photograph which is subsequently exhibited and published.

Interviews, journals, and international photographic exhibitions, have given Baudrillard a certain intellectual celebrity, a status to which he often relates in a very ambivalent manner in his reluctance to comply with the demands of journalists or photographers or exhibition organisers. At the reception in London for his book *Symbolic Exchange and Death*, he refused to pose in the daylight for photographers. At the opening of his photographic exhibition in Leicester, he refused to stop smoking, risking setting off the alarms. Baudrillard reports that in a radio interview he suddenly refused to take part:

> The presenter furious at my refusal to take part in his programme acts as though I were there, asks questions, waits, leaves a silence and says on the radio: There you have it. B. is here, but he does not wish to reply. Is that what you call a philosopher? (FCM: 43)

On the other hand he has no problems with book or poster signings, and he put on a gold lamé jacket when appearing at Whiskey Pete's Casino in Nevada (Genosko 1998: 18). All of these aspects of Baudrillard are characteristic and conform to a mixing of personal, intellectual, academic and public domains which is the very object of his current theorising.

How should the journals be read; what can they tell us? In the first place one could imagine them as several kinds of journal jumbled together: factual logbook, personal diary, notebook for ideas, and so forth. Only one of the journals has come in for sustained critical discussion, his book *America*, and then rarely for the style of writing. For Baudrillard it seems that it is not now fruitful to think of travel journals in relation to actual experiences, for writing creates its own unique world. But for readers the relationship is interesting. Is he travelling alone, what kind of story is there at a personal level beside that of the text? Questions such as these might be relevant, for example, in determining whether there is another and real meaning to some of the events reported in the text.[10] But a further question is of course just how far the journals are redrafted for publication. What items are retained and what are edited out and why? Does Baudrillard also keep a diary against which the published journal is a mythic simulacrum?

Fragments of the journals find themselves interwoven into the substantive books written at about the same time. Sometimes it is clear that the fragment is contextualised in the larger study to which it relates, but sometimes the original passage is larger than the interwoven fragment and can furnish more information on the ideas discussed in the specific study. Sometimes the fragment is simply a passing thought, undeveloped, a fleeting idea. Sometimes it is apparently personal and is a considered reflection written after an encounter, written like a scene from a short story or novella. Sometimes it is a film review, a report of a concert, an account of a lecture; thoughts on the baggage carousel at the airport (CM: 156), thoughts on travelling on the metro (CM: 174). But, without organising them in any way, Baudrillard provides observations on the cultures he visits on his travels, and the photographs he took of objects are now available. *America* is an example of materials that have been selected to form a specific focus, since he travelled there so often and spent time touring. In the *Cool Memories* series there are accounts of Australia, Latin America, Canada, European cultures, and others, revealing considerable detailed observation and reflection. *The Gulf War Did Not Take Place* is really a journal of the war he refused to visit on the ground.

Is there method in this collection of material? He himself stresses that he is not a sociologist interested in the mores and politics of peoples. He does not adopt a Marxist critical frame or class position. He is interested in surfaces, images, signs, enigmas. Thus he shows virtually no interest in the literary structure of a culture, its newpapers, its institutions: a strange reading of world cultures in terms of how he encounters their surfaces on the one hand, a kind of radical empiricism through which he delights in unexpected experiences. On the other hand, the notebooks are full of observations on the ironies and paradoxical phenomena he encounters, and reflections on theories and ideas. On a typical couple of pages from 1984 one reads of how the speed of modern life is 'like the bar of soap slipping out of your fingers in the bath'; a reference to Nietzsche and the death of God; the events of May 1968, marking the beginning of the 'disappearance of politics and history'; then notes on the building of the opera house at the Bastille – there is no 'finer memorial to commemorate the death of the revolution'; how people walk along the avenues of New York 'dissolute yet oversensitive, metaphysics with infrared lighting'; then another street, this time in Rome – 'so many people on the streets always gives the impression of a silent uprising ... everything is transformed into a silent opera, a theatrical geometry'; then finally a 'soirée in Rome' – this is a 'purely macho society, the world of showbiz ... It must be nice to live in bodies so beautiful, so ingenuous, and allow the men to dominate you with all their ugliness, wealth and pretensions. It must be marvellous to be a woman' (CM: 189).

This writing is quick, sliced, 'splintered' (BL: 203). The images come as fragments. In the bath, in Paris, in New York, in Rome, the disappearance of politics and history, the death of the revolution ... Yet there are analytical conclusions rapidly outlined. We read about Italian society: that the function of the state today is to make itself indispensable, by 'undermining all forms of spontaneous regulation ... in order to substitute its artificial mechanisms ... exactly like medicine, which lives off the destruction of natural defences and their replacement by artificial ones' (CM: 189). On the next page it seems that Baudrillard has invested in a new typewriter: 'the automatic carriage-return on the typewriter, electronic central locking on cars: these are the things that count. The rest is just theory and literature' (CM: 191). A few pages on, a rare nostalgic passage about a former lover: 'I have even forgotten her name' (CM: 205). Then an account of hearing Borges talk and saying 'Life itself is a quotation' (CM: 209).

The journals do belong to a genre of philosophically inspired notebooks, like those of Kierkegaard or Nietzsche. Baudrillard himself refers to those of Canetti, and of Gombrowicz. But the notebooks of other writers often provide rooted conversations, and a sense of the passage of time as if the journal was a record of a journey. Only the *America* notebook has this feel and has focus. The *Cool Memories* series, however, has a trajectory of its own. It begins with a five-year period, 1980 to 1985, which is rich and varied. The journal of the years 1990 to 1995 is no longer divided into years, and has just one date, May 1993 on page 65. In the first section of the book there is only a single reference to the Gulf War and his own 'cool memories' of his analysis of it, after refusing the offer to go to the Gulf as a correspondent: 'Working on the event as it happens ... yet not in real time and not with the benefit of hindsight, but with the distance of anticipation. Journalism of the third kind, the very opposite of news reporting' (FCM: 33). Gradually the referential structure of travel and the referential illusion of reality give way to the briefest allusions. The fragments become more and more abstract, puzzle-making becomes predominant, as the theme of the puzzle, the fragment and the enigma become central in Baudrillard's theorising.

Reading Baudrillard

'Master ironist who in more recent works has succumbed to it' (Scruton, 1998: 143). Baudrillard's works are certainly puzzles to reviewers, and they are sometimes treated with utter contempt – all a load of 'remarkable silliness' expressed in a form of writing which amounts to 'a thick prophylactic against understanding' (said Robert Hughes). Julie Burchill, citing Hughes, reviewed *The Transparency of Evil* for the *Sunday Times* in May 1993 and thought that 'at times, the silliness can mutate into sheer audacity and almost bring the trick off'. She admits she 'took a slight shine to him' and noticed his initials JB. The book was translated by James Benedict, who she connects with James ... Bond, and then James Brown. 'Then there's *me*': Julie Burchill. His books have titles that could be French perfumes: *Seduction*, *Cool Memories*, she notes; before claiming that at least one of Baudrillard's remarks (on the USSR in Afghanistan) was originally her own idea.

She concludes that Baudrillard is 'part visionary and part con man'. France, she says can produce people who can *talk* about pop culture even if virtually alone in Europe France cannot produce 'any pop culture of its own'.

Peter Hamilton, writing for the *Sunday Times* in December 1994, had researched the standing of Baudrillard among sociologists. Stuart Hall suggested that 'We just don't have anybody who has his sort of intellectual clout, who you could take seriously as a provocative commentator on modern society.' And Zygmunt Bauman said that Baudrillard was 'the only writer to reflect the experience of the postmodern condition, its rhythms, the uniformity of form and content, its rapidity and confusion'. Hamilton reported that a Baudrillard lecture in Australia attracted 1200 people, 'many wearing Jean Baudrillard baseball caps'.

These are baffling enigmas. Chris Horrocks reflects that 'for a writer who has been embraced by a generation of techno-nerds and media pundits, Baudrillard's discomfort with technology and computers in particular seems odd', and reports with amazement that he 'is taking his life in his hands when he admits surfing the net in search of web sites devoted to his work'. But, says Horrocks, one ignores Baudrillard at one's peril, 'for Baudrillard over the last thirty years or so, has radically altered our understanding of consumer culture and information society. He has successively knocked down, in an elegant if disturbing manner, the foundations on which we build our versions of reality.'[11]

Baudrillard is well known as a provocative thinker, who in retrospect may be acknowledged to have shown great prescience with regard to consumerism and the rise of postmodern cultures, but whose actual analyses have a level of complexity which leaves many baffled. There is confusion about whether he is serious or simply a complete impostor. There is a problem over whether he is radical or reactionary. But what is also interesting is that although Baudrillard has provided a vast number of interviews and the *Cool Memories* series, there are still mysteries about him which have never been addressed. We know nothing about his early maturity for example, apart from the fact that he fled from his studies, and never entered the *grandes écoles*. He reports having been politicised in the Algerian war period, influenced by Sartre. He wrote for Sartre's *Les Temps modernes*, but was he in the Sartre circle? Did he do military service? Born in 1929, he was almost 40 when his first book was published. During his university career some major event seems to have happened in his personal life, which is alluded to by Lotringer in his portrait of Baudrillard in 'Hyperreal' (Stearns & Chaloupka 1992: 38–42) and to which Baudrillard sometimes refers himself: 'I had the revelation that I was entering the period of the rest of my life from another point of view, in a state of complete irony with respect to what had gone before ... Somewhere along the line I stopped living ... '(BL: 104–5). What happened is obscure.

Baudrillard relates that, up to a certain point, theory was completely external to the way he lived, 'a kind of game' (BL: 105). But then this changed, when 'by various paths, all this came to have extremely direct consequences on my life' (BL: 104).

In *Fatal Strategies* there are direct illustrations of points from Baudrillard's own experiences. Even if these remain obscure in their detail, at least one interviewer has commented on them. Patrice Bollon remarked: 'I interpreted *Fatal Strategies* as a treatise on your own personal metamorphosis, a sort of Confessions of a *fin-de-siècle* intellectual.' Baudrillard in reply acknowledged that it was from that point that he had been keeping his journal which he imagined as a single book 'with parallel entries where you would have the more theoretical part on one side and the journal on the matching page. It would be a monstrous book ... like some gadget that wouldn't work' (BL: 39). There was a change from *Seduction* (1979) on, when 'everything has got intertwined ... you are in a kind of schizophrenia which may be very complex ... but you remain in a state of redoubling' (BL: 40). The crucial reference here is to Nietzsche in whose works 'the intertwining is very striking'. These remarks in this interview of 1983 reveal something of the way Baudrillard conceived the shift that was taking place:

> ... a manifesto would be like mounting a new opera ... That would need the illusion of rupture. That is what I wanted to avoid. What I was doing previously was more in the nature of a disenchanted, indifferent statement ... That remains true. Only now I envisage a sort of energy of implosion which is trying to find itself. Thus there is the possibility of an inverse energy, a departure, but I can't yet see in which direction it leads. (BL: 40)

Following Nietzsche's path meant taking steps into the dark.

Douglas Kellner also thought Baudrillard's new styles of the post-1979 period opened up 'his personal life to rather detailed inspection, in a quasi-confessional mode ... [he] confesses episodes of self-abuse while describing the ablutions of his toilet bowl, describes his sexual ecstasies with Thai prostitutes ... and in general gives us a glimpse into his everyday life' (1989: 201). Kellner refers to the French edition, but the passages are now available in the translation, to which one might turn in search of Baudrillard's confessions. The first reference is to a typical passage from *Cool Memories*:

> My sink is blocked. I pour tons of caustic soda crystals down ... A fierce struggle begins in the pipes ... A fierce bubbling and sulphurous ejaculations bear witness to the lumps of phlegm, hair, and excrement accumulated with the hygienic violence of the masturbator. And suddenly the whole thing empties. Life can go on. (CM: 150–1)

The second passage is about Thailand:

> The women of Thailand are so beautiful that they have become the hostesses of the Western world, sought after and desired everywhere for their grace, which is that of a submissive and affectionate femininity of nubile slaves – now dressed by Dior – an astounding sexual come-on ... In short the fulfilment of Western man's dreams ...What is left for [Thai] men but to assist in the universal promotion of their women for high-class prostitution? (CM: 168)

Perhaps Kellner thought he had actually read about Baudrillard's 'sexual ecstasies with Thai prostitutes' but turning to the French edition they are not to be found either. The words 'sexual come-on', 'acquiescence', 'fulfilment', 'prostitute', exist but not in the confessional order Kellner has imagined. Kellner's thesis on Baudrillard's adoption of these new styles and the intertwining of life and theoretical writing is that it is 'the ecstasy of Baudrillard himself and his disappearance in a pure state of simulation and the hyperreal' (Kellner 1989: 200), in other words the inverse of the 'hyperreal' Baudrillard imagined by Lotringer in his log cabin.

'Baudrillard hyperrealises himself and explodes in ecstasy ... triumphant accession to pure commodification and self-fetishism' (Ibid. 201) on the one hand, and 'Who else but a man of Baudrillard's caliber would pile up all his belongings in plastic bags at the bottom of the cabin?' (Lotringer, in Stearns & Chaloupka 1992: 40) on the other.

> Who are you then, J.B., you who speak of simulacra, but a simulacrum yourself?
> Answer: it is because I exist that I can advance the hypothesis of the universal simulacrum and simulation. You who are already unreal cannot envisage the unreality of things. You who are merely the shadows of yourselves cannot advance the hypothesis of transparency. (FCM: 28)

Terms

Baudrillard's texts pose certain difficulties for the reader in that they employ a specialised vocabulary of theoretical terms. There have been one or two attempts to define these. Levin has a glossary including the following terms employed by Baudrillard: Accursed Share, Anagram, Chaos Theory, Evil, Fatal Strategy, Fractal, Hyperreality, Hysteresis, Mirror, Other/Otherness, Pataphysics, Seduction, Simulacra/ Simulation, Strange Attractor (Levin 1996: 262–82). Horrocks has a very short and rather inaccurate glossary which includes Pataphysics, Strange Attractors, Metastasis, Paroxysm, Hysteresis, Accelerated Events, Recycling, Residues, Singularities, Viruses, Illusion, Ruse, Quantum, Disappearance, Simulation (Horrocks 1999: 74–7). The terms chosen by these writers reveal that Baudrillard adopts a mix of anthropological, literary, linguistic, philosophical, and psychoanalytic concepts alongside a number drawn from new areas of biology, physics and other new departures, especially in computing and information theory. Comparing the definitions provided by these two glossaries it is noticeable that they do coincide: Levin's definition of hysteresis, for example, is 'a phenomenon in which a physical effect on a body lags behind its cause' (Levin 1996: 275); Horrocks says it is 'the lagging of an effect behind a cause'. (Baudrillard, however, writes of the increasing reversibility of cause and effect (IE: 110).) But is there anything to be gained by a glossary of Baudrillardian concepts, when Baudrillard says 'no thinker who follows only the logic of his concepts has ever seen farther than the end of his nose' (FS: 73)?

Why is that? It is because the

> rational systems of morality, value, science, reason command only the linear evolution of societies, their visible history. But the deeper energy comes from elsewhere. From prestige, challenge, from all the seductive or antagonistic impulses, including suicidal ones, which have nothing to do with a social morality or a morality of history or progress. (FS: 72–3).

This idea provides a clue to the general shape of Baudrillard's idea of theory: it is to overturn the presupposition that modern Western culture, and particularly the Enlightenment, derives its force from reason and logic. The vital, dynamic and vibrant cultures are articulated in an altogether different manner, just as radical theorising is never simply the application of logical principles.

On the other hand, Baudrillard's thought is evidently not random or incoherent, but quite the contrary: it is rigorous with high degrees of conceptual consistency. It is not based on an appeal to mystical inner revelation, or to a pure personal experience. Baudrillard is also quite insistent that he does not work towards the elaboration of a doctrine, but of a strategy (BL: 81). The encounter is not with a 'spatial other, but the form of alterity' (P: 41). The construction of an exhaustive Baudrillardian glossary would tend to consolidate doctrine over strategy, or to turn strategy into doctrine or method. Some recent interpretations have read Baudrillard's theoretical work as unchanging (for example, Butler 1999), but what strikes the attentive reader are the discontinuities, and the remarkable experimentation and play, in this body of writing. Baudrillard does occasionally appeal to a radical empiricism of experience against ridiculously out of date concepts. Experience is never purely empirical in Baudrillard, however: it encounters a fatal strategy that is certainly conjunctural, provisional, and conjectural.

> He does not define concepts, he does not analyse them,
> he does not criticise them: he murders them
> (but the crime is never perfect). (FCM: 77)

CHAPTER 2

Overview

> It is the power of the object which cuts
> a swathe through every artifice we have
> imposed on it. (PC: 74)

This chapter provides a brief account of Baudrillard's writing and the way his ideas have developed over three decades. It identifies the key shifts in his thought and the emergence of new themes in a diverse body of work which nonetheless reveals a persistent attempt to think about what he calls the 'object' – 'that's what I was obsessed with from the start' (BL: 24).

Trajectory

His first book was entitled *The System of Objects* (1968), and in it he outlined a theory of the 'object system'. He defined this as the conjunction of the system of commodities and the system of signs: what others have analysed as the process of reification and alienation became for Baudrillard a general semiological process which marked the last phase of an alienated society. His next book *The Consumer Society* (1970) provided a general account of the affluent society in which consumption, not production, is its dominant mechanism. But by *La Gauche divine* (1985) he thought that even a consumerism characterised by alienation and spectacular consumption had given way to a new glacial, non-spectacular form dominated by information technology and fractal culture (GD: 144) in which the significance of the 'object' had been radically transformed. Thus Baudrillard's writings seem to chart the evolution of modernity into postmodernity; indeed, he has been called 'the author of postmodern culture and society' (Kroker & Cook 1988). Although he draws on sociology, his most important philosophical influence is Nietzsche. In 1987 he published a short intellectual autobiography, *L'Autre par lui-même* (in English as *The Ecstasy of Communication*), perhaps the best short introduction to his work to that date. He claims no longer to adopt the tragic vision entailed in the critique of modernity but rather a melancholy attitude – 'let us be stoics' (EC: 101).[1]

His earliest writings included a thesis on Nietzsche; he was the principal translator of the works of Peter Weiss into French; he was a teacher of German in *lycées* before taking up a position in sociology at Paris University (Nanterre) in 1966. His early essays are dominated by an effort to develop a critical structuralism, in projects directly influenced by both Henri Lefebvre and Roland Barthes. But in his third book, *For a Critique of the Political Economy of the Sign* (originally 1972), and even more *The Mirror of Production* (originally 1973), he moves decisively to change the basis of his position away from that of a traditional concept of class struggle to that of opposing the symbolic order to the semiotic (or simulation) order constituent of contemporary Western culture. The first result of posing this opposition was his study *Symbolic Exchange and Death* (originally 1976), followed by *Seduction* (1979), *Simulacra and Simulation* (1981), *Fatal Strategies* (1983), *The Transparency of Evil* (1990), *The Illusion of the End* (1992). In his brief intellectual autobiography he suggests that – beginning with *Seduction* – he no longer engages in a critique of modernity from the point of view of symbolic exchange but takes up the position of the object, now a 'pure sign' which carries a fatal, objective irony (EC: 90). In his later fractal stage, even this effectivity of the sign disappears as he has come to take up the side of the 'cosmic order'. With great inner consistency his styles of writing changed to embrace the challenge of the symbolic: the poetic (*L'Ange de stuc*, 1978) and the aphoristic and fragmented (the *Cool Memories* series). It is arguable that his work never really abandons the idea that symbolic exchange constitutes a superior cultural formation to that of Western rationalism and post-rationalism, or to put it even more strongly, that ultimately the inner structures of Western culture have never been able to escape the dynamic of symbolic exchange (see *Forget Foucault*), and yet remain incapable of developing a genuinely symbolic superstructure themselves. In his more recent writings, particularly *The Perfect Crime* (1995) and *Impossible Exchange* (1999), Baudrillard has sought to identify some of the more extreme paradoxes in contemporary culture.

From Marx to Nietzsche

Baudrillard's analysis of capitalist society in his first two books was a highly original version of critical social theory. Very much against the trend of orthodox Marxism or Althusserianism however, he insisted on the decisive novelty of affluence and the way in which consumerism had become the dominant feature of social integration in class-divided societies. Instead of achieving social and class integration through the discipline of work and economic production, the dominant means of achieving this was now through the activities of consumption, consumer culture, and leisure. He applied Barthes' semiological method to the analysis of objects and combined this with what he called a theory of the 'structural law of value'. This was an enlargement of Marx's notion of the law of value, or rather Marx's theory was now seen as a particular application of a more general process which could be identified in many distinct spheres of culture. Whereas Barthes' analysis of fashion was essentially formal, Baudrillard's was critical – emphasising the fact that fashion could invade and restructure any aspect of society, including philosophy, as modular element (the formation of a combinatory system) and as modal temporality (the fashion cycle). Both aspects were seen by Baudrillard as 'semiological reductions' – assaults on a vital symbolic culture. In his critique of Marxism (in the *Mirror of Production*) he argued that Marx had not really understood this relationship but had merely analysed the reduction of exchange-value to use-value. In an analysis which has important consequences if correct, use-value was shown to be already produced by semiological culture, which itself presupposes utility. Thus Marxism had not been radical enough to escape the logic of capitalist exchange itself. In addition, structuralism, applied in anthropology, naively projected semiotic reason backwards on to primitive societies – an inappropriate method which could at best end only in radical misunderstanding, reinforcing a fundamental contempt for other cultures.

Baudrillard's analysis of symbolic exchange, inspired by Marcel Mauss and Georges Bataille, established the divergence between potlatch and political economy, gift exchange and commodity exchange, seasonal cycles and capital accumulation. At first Baudrillard contrasted the ambivalence of the symbol against the univocality of the sign. But as his work developed he was able to establish further aspects of symbolic cultures which collectively created a sharp contrast with Western culture: ritual, eternal recurrence, sacrifice, life–death cycle, seduction, reversibility, destiny, and evil. At the most extreme, he argued that primitive societies were not societies in that they did not 'produce' and did not 'consume', in fact did not 'exchange'. Such concepts, developed in Western philosophy, are dependent on basic notions current within bourgeois society, even (and not least) the fundamental concept of 'mode of production'. At this time Baudrillard began to adopt a Nietzschean perspective in which Western culture is seen as an emergent slave morality of *ressentiment*, plagued by a tragic inversion of values, against which a process of cultural struggle may produce an affirmative transvaluation. The assertion of *amor fati* against *ressentiment* is the theme of Baudrillard's *Fatal Strategies*; the assertion of the principle of seduction against that of production is the theme of the book *Seduction*. However, there seem to be limits to Baudrillard's Nietzscheanism: although he refuses the Christian notion of individual responsibility and subjective guilt, he specifically rejects any possibility of transcending the principle of evil. Indeed he stresses that the symbolic order of good and evil 'transcends us totally' and should be 'accepted totally' (TE: 109). This leads Baudrillard to a fundamental acceptance of Bataille's notion of the accursed share, and links Baudrillard to the central tradition of German moral thought exemplified by Goethe and Hölderlin.

Seduction is the work that marked the turning point in his writing as far as style and position were concerned. Here the main points of reference are no longer sociology, but art, philosophy, and literature; Borges, Kafka, and Kierkegaard. Baudrillard creates a genealogy for seduction parallel to that established by Walter Benjamin for the work of art: first, a stage of ritual – 'the anonymity of the artist'; second, a stage of individual production of the work of art which carries the mark of individuality and an aesthetic dimension in a system shorn of obligation; and third, the work of art in the period of its mechanical reproducibility. Seduction likewise has its initial ritual phase, based on the relation of the duel. This is followed by an aesthetic phase where the exemplar for Baudrillard is Kierkegaard's seducer (*Diary of a Seducer*) who elaborates an ironic strategy of seduction as an art. This passes into the third 'political' form where seduction is maximally dispersed as a social form of solicitation while being deprived of all intensity and content; Baudrillard's formula for this phase is: maximal circulation with minimal intensity. Baudrillard then transposes this again into a new threefold classification: first, the phase of the duel/dual relation (the object of ritual transformation established by the dominance of the rule); second, the stage of the law, of polarity where the relation is one of dialectic or contract. This passes into a third form where the relation has become a connection determined by the immanence of digitality and models. In this latter phase seduction becomes cool, becomes an ambience.

There is, however, a strong Nietzschean allusion (to 'How the "Real World" at last Became a Myth', *Twilight of the Idols*) in 'The Precession of Simulacra' (in *Simulacra and Simulation*), which constitutes Baudrillard's attempt to replace the concept of semiology with notions of simulation first discussed in *Symbolic Exchange and Death* (part 2). This important discussion is a basis for Baudrillard's own solution to the Marxist problem of ideology and indeed for a new periodisation of Western culture beyond that established in relation to seduction. There are a number of orders of simulacra in this new genealogy. The first order, which dominated European culture from the Renaissance to the eighteenth century, is exemplified by the *trompe l'oeil* (the enchanted moment of simulacra), and the automaton in manufacture; this is a system of simulacra corresponding to small craft enterprises. Here simulation entails postulating an original work or object of which the copy is its counterfeit. The poetic work *L'Ange de stuc*, is an evocation of the ambience of this world (its prose version can be found in SED: 50–3 and in S: 60–6). Baudrillard also calls it the 'natural' stage of simulacra – corresponding to a pre-industrial stage of use-value.

The second order of simulacra corresponds to the industrial system and the machine. Here it is mass production which establishes the equivalence of a series of manufactured products. This system is one of reproduction in the absence of any true or natural original from which the series is reproduced. The utopias of this period are promethean – corresponding to the dominant ethos of history, dialectic, progression, revolution. This is the period of the emerging hegemony of science which aims to abolish the world of appearances, to expose and master the real. It is, therefore, for Baudrillard, the 'golden age of alienation', of exchange-value and its critique, and later of surrealism in art.

The third order corresponds to the communication revolution, the dominance of codes and the mass media. In this period the key form is genetic reproduction through aleatory commutation. This marks an end to dialectic, history, and revolution. This form of simulation goes beyond any relation of representation: it is that which is always already reproduced. Instead of surrealism in art, here reality itself becomes hyperreal in the aestheticisation of reality through sign-value, media, and computer models. These establish 'the blind but brilliant ambience of simulacra' (SED: 75). At this stage, radicality passes from the alienated subject and installs itself in the objective passion of the object. Here the subject classes adopt a fatal silent strategy of hyper-conformity, a new post-revolutionary form of resistance; this time the masses are object.

There is a fourth order which Baudrillard calls the fractal stage, or viral stage, or the 'irradiated stage of value': here value 'radiates in all directions, filling in all interstices, without bearing reference to anything whatsoever except by mere contiguity' (in Stearns & Chaloupka 1992: 15). This stage also seems to mark the end of the period where the disappearance of things occurs through a finite death or 'fatal mode' of return; so here the dominant form is where things are simply and indifferently proliferated and dispersed into the void (Ibid. 12). This fourth, fractal, stage corresponds to a world dominated by transpolitical forms, the transaesthetic, transeconomic, transproductive, transsexual, and so on, and the virtual economic slump, the virtual (Gulf) war. When culture has rejected all its negative components, it becomes a closed system, it becomes virtual and open to a pathology of the code: to anomaly and metastasis. Unlike the pathologies of earlier stages, such as mechanical system failure or anomie, the new pathology is strangely aestheticised and relates specifically to bodies that have become purged of internal negative principles; these are 'virtual bodies' with gravely weakened immune systems.

Modernity

Baudrillard has thus developed what might be called a general theory of Western social and cultural modernisation. This was first offered as a critical theory of capitalist affluence, focusing on the system of objects as a form of social alienation. The basis of criticism shifted to symbolic exchange, from which were elaborated a series of polarities: sign–

symbol, production–seduction, and so on. The focus shifted again to examining the transition from history to the features of the societies dominated by third- and fourth-order simulation: here Baudrillard found not a principle of critique, of negation as such, but a principle of evil (carried by the object), and an 'unprecedented pathology'. In charting this scenario of the genealogy of resistance and opposition, class struggle was clearly located in the promethean phase of production and bourgeois revolution, the hot explosive phase of historical dialectic. The phase dominated by the code turns cultural evolution into an implosive mode: critical opposition to the code, like all negativity, even the proletariat itself, is simply absorbed into the cultural system and neutralised. It is as if, Baudrillard suggests, the only revolutionary class had been the bourgeoisie which, in establishing bourgeois society, in effect ushered in a post-alienated and classless society, but one quite unlike that envisaged by Marx.

Yet the way in which 'the culture of the West' developed is by no means uniform. The clearest difference is between Europe and America. America, he argues, seems to have missed the whole experience of the second order of simulation, to have passed directly from the eighteenth to the twentieth century. Its culture was already hyperreal, and Baudrillard always insists it is a contradiction of an achieved utopia. American culture therefore knows no internal dissidence or deep irony. The positive banality of American culture, however, is always mythic, permanently dreamlike in character. European culture anticipates reality by imagining it; American culture – and this is its defining characteristic – refuses this order. That is why European culture struggles to adapt to modernity, while America lives it extravagantly. Europe has never become modern (a thesis others have developed without acknowledging its Baudrillardian source); it conserves its high culture. America produced no such articulation. Disneyland is a pure expression of this logic, and as such struggles to survive in Europe, where it is semiotically inauthentic. Baudrillard's basic image for American culture is that of the desert, and in exchange for the beauty of the desert it would be good to sacrifice a woman. If the image of such a sacrifice seems bizarre or even gratuitous, it is consistent with the logic of symbolic exchange which continues to haunt *America*. But it should not obscure the fact that this essay, along with *Cool Memories*, seems to open the door to a positive comparative analysis of cultures. Much of the comparison so far initiated in his writing is between France and America, but there are striking references to the specificity of the symbolic strength of Italian, Mexican, and Japanese cultures. It is perhaps against this background that Baudrillard's essays on the Gulf War should be read. His writing strives to capture the specificity of Islamic cultures, the singularity of the Iranian revolution, and the symbolic *fatwa* against Salman Rushdie. With Saddam Hussein's strategy, however, the use of hostages has lost its symbolic power, and his calculated practices have become complicit with those of the West. The war in its Western experience was virtual, entirely displaced now into media images and simulation of war: for Baudrillard in fact a war can no longer take place in the West – except virtually – once third- and fourth-order simulations dominate cultural forms.

Western culture cannot tolerate the radical alterity of other cultures. Humanism, the doctrine of universal human rights with its assumption of human equality, like evangelical Christianity, seeks to form the world after its own image and thus reduces radical otherness to domesticated 'differences'. The result is the imperialist process of the homogenisation of world culture: the world-wide assault on symbolic cultures. This process also paradoxically creates a new racism and sexism, phenomena which belong strictly to a culture which cannot tolerate radical alterity. In developing his theories, Baudrillard opts for the position of the radical other, that which is 'more than other', the object conceived as a 'strange attractor', that which permits an escape from alienation but only into absolute exoticism. From this position the media-dominated culture of the West can appear as the 'ecstasy of communication'.

In fact this formulation may well be too condensed to do full justice to Baudrillard's latest writings, which suggest that the age of the struggle for human rights itself belonged to the period of the alienation of the subject and to the period in which subjective criticism could be effective and have some meaning. We have passed from the alienated individual to a new postmodern individualism, a form Baudrillard theorises as an unprecedented structure of auto-servitude. His writings on this subject are among his most brilliant, yet they involve the most difficult and subtle changes of position in his work. His thesis is that 'at all events, it is better to be controlled by someone other than by oneself. Better to be oppressed, exploited, persecuted and manipulated by someone other than by oneself', in what he calls the 'declination of wills' (TE: 167). The logic of this reversal is taken to its extreme conclusion: 'the entire movement for liberation and emancipation, in as much as it is predicated on a demand for greater autonomy – or, in other words, on a more complete introjection of all forms of control and constraint under the banner of freedom – is a regression' (TE: 167). He advocates a new ethic 'founded on the transmission of foreignness' (TE: 168). But how does this correspond to the new conjuncture?

Forms of resistance

Baudrillard suggests that at each stage various modes of resistance are provoked. At the moment of production and alienation, the subject sought to find a transcendence of alienation in revolution. In the later stages of simulation this mode is absorbed, and the dominant forms of resistance become ironic modes of conformity and withdrawal (a new strategy of the object). As the separation of the subject and object is problematised and dissolves across the sciences, Baudrillard introduces the term *hyperreal* for the resultant transformation of the ontological status of the object. Instead of the emergence of a featureless culture of late modernity, he imaginatively proposes a culture of uniformity combined with heightened effects and extreme phenomena. Marxist conceptions of overdetermined contradiction, ideological class struggle and hegemonic strategies are no longer capable of providing an analysis of the world brought about by science and post-industrial technology.

Baudrillard developed a programme in which terms like *production* and *exploitation* were replaced by *seduction* and *excommunication*, a move from economic to cultural analysis, and from production to 'impossible exchange'. Baudrillard's analyses of the primacy of gift over commodity was provocative: capitalism is driven not by the logic of capitalist accumulation but by a profound disruption of gift exchange. The gift of work cannot be returned by the labourer, and therein lies the crisis of modern society. Symbolic exchange is rendered impossible within the structures of commodity exchange and capital accumulation. There is a further consequence: the way that capitalism is transformed introduces an 'uncertainty surrounding the reality of the crisis' (SED: 33). In this context the proletariat is not only corrupted as agent, it is also integrated and neutralised through its commitment to values derived from production and use. In opposition to a struggle on the level of real exploitation, Baudrillard sought a level of counter-symbolic gift which the system could not return.

Baudrillard's analysis of death (SED: 126), through a long study of its genealogical forms, was undoubtedly influenced by Foucault's genealogy of madness, a project also interested in excommunication rather than exploitation. Baudrillard suggests that the first and fundamental form of exclusion, that from which all others are derived, is that of the dead. First the dead are retained in the community. When the dead are excluded from the community and interred in the necropolis or the cemetery, the separation of body and soul is reflected in a social struggle over the destiny of the soul of the departed. What interests Baudrillard here is the changing value and significance of life as determined by the meaning of death (just as madness determines the meaning of reason).

At the moment he completed this study in 1976, Foucault's book *Discipline and Punish* (Foucault 1977) appeared. Baudrillard's violent critique of this work proposed that Foucault had abandoned the symbolic framework of his earlier studies: 'Forget Foucault' was his immediate response (*Forget Foucault*). Baudrillard's view was that Foucault had adopted, in a significant theoretical change of position, a conception of power as accumulation, as omnipresent, as productive. Against this view Baudrillard wrote of new forms of resistance in contemporary society through hyper-conformity, silence as a fatal strategy, indifference as passion, power as essentially reversible.

If the essay *Seduction* (1979) charts the genealogy of seduction through three stages (the rule, the law and the norm), the question arises of how this maps on to the orders of simulacra. The first form of seduction is characterised by the logic of the duel, the second by the dialectical logic of polarities, while the third is characterised by a digital connection. In the first, a ritual culture of the rule is one where the passionate involvement in the theatre of ceremonial produces a form of play which retains vital symbolic spaces between actors. In the second, the society based on law and contract is also that of contradiction, transgression and revolution. The third is the era of cold tactile seduction; of models, simulation, information, and the self-seduction of cloning. The brief historical sketch which accompanies this genealogy identifies the masses as object in two phases: first, the period of alienation when the masses were violently oppressed, and when subjects attempted to transcend this situation in revolutionary mass action; second, the period in which the masses, in conditions of high consumption and political democracy, 'are rigged out' with subjective desires so that they might enter the commercial game of seduction (economic and political). Without this shift in the system, the integration of the masses in third-order simulacra would fail, and the political system would find itself in a continuous and increasingly impossible search for legitimacy.

Developing his thesis on seduction in this way, Baudrillard inevitably encounters modern feminism and the thesis that his notion of the culture of seduction is a patriarchal trap and an oppressive form for women. Baudrillard's position in reply is that modern feminism, like Foucault's theory of power, not only gets caught in the trap of the 'real' of contemporary culture and politics, but engenders it in the same way as traditional proletarian action engenders the real around production. The moment sexual liberation is taken up by feminism as a liberation of women's sexuality, it falls into the game of the realisation of sex. In the symbolic order, the feminine is in a duel/dual relationship with the masculine, which it challenges to exist. The categories of feminine and masculine in such cultures are not simple structural categories: they are forms which attract each other, and exist in a fatal order of symbolic metamorphosis. In contemporary culture, this duality is reduced to a set of ludic differences, real exchanges in which the very terms masculine and feminine begin to lose their individual definition. What was previously a drama of sexual passion, the cruel seduction of the object, becomes soft play in a safe ambience. At the end of the essay on seduction, Baudrillard concludes by insisting on the fundamental primacy of the primitive form: that if 'everything is driven by seduction, it would not be by this soft seduction ... but by a defiant seduction, a dual, antagonistic seduction with the stakes maximised' (SS: 178).

Fatal theory

From the moment Baudrillard adopted the position of symbolic exchange, his writing was divided between the essay and the fragment, analysis and poetry. He appeared to adopt the position of the most extreme points of modernity and the most archaic modes of symbolic cultures. These styles of writing were never given a separate and specific methodological reflection, though they are undoubtedly profoundly systematic and even highly rationalistic. Baudrillard's explicit aim in opposing mysticism and rationalism is not, however, to make discoveries about new objects. Such strategies are naive and constantly surprised by ironic outcomes. Theory, for Baudrillard, must take account of the failures of conventional positivist theory by anticipating the ironic power of its object in advance. Instead of trying to master the object, or unveil its truth, theory must challenge and seduce the object in its turn. In this strategy the aim is no longer one of disenchantment, but quite the reverse. Thus the key injunction to the power of theory is to say to the enigma that confronts it, return a no less enigmatic reply. If the world is no longer trapped in a dialectical logic and unfolds exponentially, theory must raise the level of its own stakes. If the world is paradoxical, theory must be even more paradoxical.

Baudrillard's surprising strategy is no longer conceived as a project of a knowing subject, but as *fatal* and ironic itself. Baudrillard provides not only a theory of the semiotic stages of Western culture, but also a new way of relating to this theory. Thus as his writings suggest new analyses of simulation, transpolitical forms, virtual cultures, his relation to them is not a critical rationalism. His writing attempts to provoke a paradoxical counter-spiral. And the distance between the two spirals is precisely that of the ritual, the symbolic relation, not one of mastery or possession or *ressentiment*. The major temptations here, and ones which Baudrillard consciously tries to avoid, are firstly, to replace the infrastructure–superstructure conception of the social formation with the symbolic order replacing the economy as the base in a system of overdetermined contradictions, and secondly to produce a nostalgic vision based on a sentimental idea of 'the world we have lost' as a new form of *ressentiment*.

What Baudrillard manages to achieve is a way of theorising as a radical other to positive and critical theory. In this sense, it is not so much his writing on the modernisation and postmodernisation of Western cultures which is significant, but the elaboration and practice (if that is still the right word) of theory which is external to these processes and remains at the same time their secret. Here, then, is the most fundamental surprise Baudrillard suggests: it is not modernity which is active and dynamic, either as science, technology, rationalism, or capital accumulation. The rationalising cultures of modernity are driven, paradoxically, by the logic of a more primordial culture, the eternal return, human vulnerability, at the same time setting out in another direction towards immortality and perfection. Baudrillard theorises this as the collapse of a culture into the banal illusion of the world, the brilliant cultures of destiny and predestination collapse into their residues – banal chance and chaos. As he charts the evolution of Western cultures he follows a course which parallels Lyotard's sketch of the 'postmodern condition' arising out of a revolution in the sciences (from the Newtonian to the Einsteinian universe). Baudrillard's reading of this transition is that it is only with the displacement of the order of destiny in a society that the shift towards the aleatoric cosmic order can occur. The outcome is highly paradoxical: on the one hand, the logic of chaos and fractal theory arises out of the annihilation of the fatal and predestined; on the other, it arises only as a result of the strange power of seduction of objects dispersed into the void. In his more recent writings Baudrillard seems to pay much more attention to the radical idea of the cosmic order in this sense than to the symbolic order.

It is because of the complexity of this position that Baudrillard is drawn to and repulsed by the development of postmodern theory. On the one hand, his analysis traces the evolution of modern and postmodern science and follows Lyotard in conceiving this development as moving from a science of discovery to a science of paralogy. But he does not follow Deleuze in appropriating the reality of the aleatoric because the 'postmodern' order is a false resolution to a progressive sequence: driven by seduction in the strong and antagonistic sense, it produces a general culture of seduction in the soft and ludic sense. Thus even Baudrillard's fatal strategy, which reintroduces radical theoretical alterity into the analysis of objects, seems to play into a dynamic of self-contradictory effects.

Two concluding observations. Firstly, his position on the latest phase of simulation, the fractal phase, does seem to mark a considerable shift in his relation to Nietzsche, for here the

> very possibility of the Eternal Return is becoming precarious: that marvellous perspective presupposes that things unfold in a necessary predestined order, the sense of which lies beyond them. There is nothing like that today; things merely disperse in a randomness that leads nowhere. Today's Eternal Return is that of the infinitely small, the fractal, the obsessive repetition of things on a microscopic and inhuman scale. It is not the exaltation of a will, nor the sovereign affirmation of an event, nor its consecration by an immutable sign – such as Nietzsche's thought – but the viral recurrence of microprocesses. (A: 72–3)

And according to the thesis of the accursed share, anything that purges evil in its own structures signs its own death warrant (TE: 106).

The second observation is that one of the most remarkable aspects of this work is the development of a general conception of a primitive, or rather a primal, culture – what he has called the order of 'symbolic exchange'. Initially this order was essentially ambivalent, and impossible to frame within a structural semiological matrix without disfiguring it entirely. Gradually this seeming 'ambivalence' was given greater and greater definition involving ideas of seduction, fate, reversible time, and death. On the other hand, Western culture became the object of a number of brilliant genealogical studies organised around the four stages of simulation. Baudrillard has claimed that his position changed, and that from *Seduction* (1979) he abandoned as nostalgic the idea that there could ever be a return to the symbolic order, and from that moment he embraced the destiny of the object. However, it seems apparent that he could never let go of his nostalgia for this 'lost object' (EC: 80), even as at the same time he embraced the most extreme positions of hyper-modernity. This makes his writing both more conservative and more radical than that of any other cultural critic.

CHAPTER 3

Vulnerability

> The anxiety of any kind of commentary, even a
> favourable one, comes from the obscure sense
> of the skeletons in the cupboard ... (FCM: 73)

So not the least of Baudrillard's challenges to sociology was the fact that after a grounding first in literature (in the 1950s) and then in sociology (in the 1960s), he suddenly altered course (in the mid-1970s) and began writing in new styles (a social poetics) as if he had stopped reading, at least the literature of the social sciences. The opposition, tension, contrast between positive analysis and literary analysis became a central feature of his theory and his way of writing; the social theory provides the stable basis of the identification of forms, the poetic/philosophical provides the basis for critical and fatal strategies for investigating and contesting them. There is then an internal division, a systematic stylistic doubling (form and mirror), a self–other tension in this work, which condenses the very topics, issues and objects Baudrillard wants to analyse.

Simulacra

Effectively the essays written for the journal *Traverses* (and collected in *Simulacra and Simulation*) avoid all resort to referencing and empirical substantiation. But it would be a serious mistake to think these essays were not replete with sociological and philosophical language that comes through from Baudrillard's formative period. If he preferred here to engage with Kafka, Borges, Canetti, Gombrowicz, it was still within a framework established on the basis of Marx, Nietzsche, Freud, Saussure, Mauss, Bataille, Caillois, Lacan, McLuhan. If his writing remained focused on the nature and character of contemporary Western culture and its destiny, the way in which the component parts of his approach came together was so unusual among theorists that it was very easy to mistake the resultant position. In fact there is as yet no analysis of Baudrillard's writing which is adequate or altogether convincing. The real problem has been the temptation either to make a premature critique which simply misses its target by striking at the first objectionable idea – failing to see the complex theory as a whole and therefore leaving it effectively unexamined –

or, to start from a sympathetic reading of a single theme but to fail to grasp the whole.

The basic matrix of fiction theory, as outlined in the previous chapter, is articulated on the opposition between the symbolic and the semiotic (or simulacral) cultures. In effect the later writings continue and deepen Baudrillard's first essays on this opposition: on the one hand, the aspects of the symbolic which are developed in the later works are the principle of evil, alterity and radical illusion; on the other, the orders of simulation have also been extended: 'After the natural stage, the mercantile stage, and the structural stage, comes the fractal stage of value' (Baudrillard, in Stearns & Chaloupka 1992: 15). It would be tempting, of course, to call this the 'postmodern' stage (and Baudrillard at one point tempts us to think this), but it is significant that he does not in fact do this. It is also interesting that at one time Baudrillard described the relationship between the symbolic and the semiotic as a double spiral (EC: 79); but in his subsequent work, he says they come into contact like tectonic plates: where they collide, reality is subducted into the abyss (PC: 97). This seems to be a significant new image. And there is another. Where previously it could be thought that the site of the destruction of the symbolic by the semiotic order was the crucial apocalyptic scene, Baudrillard now writes that it is today reality which is the site of the 'apocalypse of simulation'.

Baudrillard's attitude to simulation and to his own work on simulation is curious. He remarks that simulation was once something that was thrown down as a challenging idea to naively reductive modern culture. Subsequently, however, the challenge has been absorbed; indeed, 'simulation' even became fashionable, and so the challenge evaporated. Baudrillard refers to the fact that the idea has merged with the real: the critical distance has been eroded and the possibility of a play between the two lost. But some other changes in Baudrillard's reflection may be linked to this. At the time he wrote *Fatal Strategies*, that is around 1980, Baudrillard argued that radicalism had passed from the subject to the object, that is to the event; however, in *The Illusion of the End*, that is around 1992, the historical event has also evaporated. Another transition can be seen, perhaps, in the shift from a situation in which he asserts he can say anything without a response (he would like to be a 'Rushdie of the Left' (BL: 169)), to a situation in which he reports a regime of complete prohibition against radical thought (PC: 105). He seems again willing to throw down the challenge of the fictional non-event from the imagined 'stealth agency': a kind of inversion of Michel Foucault's search for truth on the ground. Baudrillard suggests 'gathering news of unreal events in order to disinform the public' (IE: 14) in a practice that sustains its links with situationism and ethnomethodology but goes far beyond them both in frivolity, humour, absurdity and in (unintended) pathos.

What might these shifts be related to? One possible answer is the response he received to his writing on the GulfWar. In *The Illusion of the End* he sustains his basic judgement to question the reality of the war: 'Analysis must not be sacrificed to the expression of anger. It has to be directed in its entirety against reality ... ' (IE: 63). Of course this brought Baudrillard into a considerable amount of derision in France and elsewhere. And this has left its mark on him: 'If you say: "this war is a simulacrum", everyone bursts out laughing. Forced laughter, or condescending or convulsive laughter, as though it were a puerile joke or an obscene proposal' (PC: 95). Instead of the respected opponent, even if in the mode of the evil enemy, he became something of the ridiculed insider. The problem perhaps is that *The Illusion of the End* and *The Perfect Crime* are not as symbolically powerful as *The GulfWar Did Not Take Place*, a work of theory-fiction which has be read as paradigmatically Baudrillardian: Baudrillard against Goliath, against Leviathan, against the West. And one which re-established the radical charge of his theory of simulation by setting up, in his own words, 'against simulation a radical desimulation' (IE: 15).

Illusion

What kind of theory and challenge was this? In his recent discussions Baudrillard has put his ambition clearly on showing the superiority of the fatal and radical illusion of the world over the illusory power of the real (IE: 94). The basic inspiration is Nietzschean but with a specific continuation: 'The boundaries of the human and the inhuman are indeed blurring, yet they are doing so in a movement not towards the superhuman, but towards the subhuman' (IE: 95). Not a transvaluation of values beyond good and evil therefore, but one on 'this side' of good and evil. The basic problem is not a material one, not one of material environment or conditions of survival, but of symbolic loss. Yet Baudrillard makes sure that he is not to be misunderstood as an idealist, for what happens never comes as a result of an idea (CMII: 1). Yet it also seems false to claim that this theory entails a 'new concept of cultural materialism' (on the jacket of *Simulacra and Simulation*). He claimed it would be absurd to attempt to reconstruct a symbolic culture (in Stearns & Chaloupka 1992: 296) and that he was caught in a 'radical ambiguity' between simulation and seduction (Ibid. 298). The secret behind his ability to theorise such a bewildering array of objects in this way was the firm basis which his dichotomous theory provides for him, and his powers of imaginative inversion, reversion, invention of phenomena in relation to it. In other words, he knew what he was looking for even if, especially if, it remained strange, bizarre, extreme: he simply pushed the analysis in all directions one degree further than the reader expects (calling the outcome a *stratégie du pire*, an ecstasy). His justification for this was that it is only in this way that the current trends in the world could be theorised, since the world now is one which has passed through liberation to a complete and catastrophic liberalisation and deregulation (IE: 107). He has prepared the way for this method by introducing (in the *Cool Memories* series) a variety of language games and thought experiments, theory-fictional poetics which themselves contain the practical elements of his way of approaching objects in the world. Thus we find the striking contrast of a firm and relatively stable basic theory on the one hand (symbolic exchange versus simulacral precession), and a remarkably inventive and varied, almost completely unstable, charting of extreme phenomena on the other. On the one side, a basic unsentimental conception of the symbolic, which always provides a basic contrast; on the other side, a radical tracing of the extreme instances of the ecstatic destruction of the symbolic by the orders of the real and hyperreal (which are in the process of triumphant self-destruction – the perfect crime). One might call it Baudrillard's metaphysical pathos of simulation and desimulation, and *Cool Memories* charts the ways in which he reinvents himself as extreme witness to it. Baudrillard insisted that the opposing modalities (or rather media: either symbolic or semiotic) cannot be converted into each other: they are, as it were, fated to encircle one another, the symbolic attempting to seduce the semiotic, the semiotic trying to reduce the symbolic. The theorist has to work in two modes, the poetic and the scientific (in Stearns & Chaloupka 1992: 15).

The great virtue of Baudrillard's work was not that it concentrated on the notion of the object, but that it radicalised profoundly the notion of a critique of the object and the sign from the point of view of symbolic exchange. But this gave rise to much misinterpretation. Thus it is common to find that commentators referred to Baudrillard's mix of profound and trivial, of his interest in language games, in 'undecidables', in the fatal–banal opposition, and so on. Much of the unnecessary confusion would be dispelled if it had been made clear that the paradoxes, the inversions, flashes of wit, condensations and displacements which Baudrillard likes to experiment with and calls generically the anagrammatic, are instances of reversions, loops, non-linear, non-accumulative poetic forms. There was a basic query. How did Baudrillard conceive the symbolic order: was it graspable as seduction in all the orders and their doubles? What was the nature of the order referred to at the end of *The Illusion of the End* – 'perhaps, deep down, history has never unfolded in a linear fashion ... but as a poetic reversibility'? Against the illusion of the end, the 'illusion of our history', he poses 'the greatly more radical illusion of the world' (IE: 122). Baudrillard appeared to be in the process of searching out and finding an inventory of non-linear forms, from the simple palindrome to the general theory of the eternal return, and of discovering the divisions in this order of forms. In this respect his recent works have titles which are not really what they seem: *The Illusion of the End* was a collection of essays on time, finality, linear progressions and regressions, historic events and non-events, contrasted with that of symbolic reversibility; *The Perfect Crime* was a collection on the utopian illusion of perfection in modern technical culture, contrasted with a world of vulnerable beings. (In an interview on French Television (*Arte,* 16 April 1994) Baudrillard expressed this opposition as one between the logic of a technical culture and the vulnerable human order.) In this way Baudrillard is entirely consistent with his previous essays, all of which are studies of such oppositions (seduction–production, and so on), and consistent in the idea that far from simply bemoaning the fact of the destruction of the higher order of the symbolic in a reactionary posture, he actively affirms the process in a way which seeks (certainly not altogether successfully) to get beyond all *ressentiment* ("'push what is collapsing" said Nietzsche' (SS: 157)).

Sociology?

Certainly one of the most important contributions of Baudrillard's theorising was to challenge the hegemony of the concept of ideology within sociological analysis. This was particularly clear with the publication of *Simulacra and Simulation*. The essays cover many topics: hypermarkets, sci-fi, film reviews, a review of Ballard's *Crash*, media effects, an important essay on the architecture of the Pompidou Centre; there are also essays on advertising, May 1968 and the university, and the fate of animals. This collection revealed the scope of Baudrillard's theorising: economic, political, cultural, sexual, literary, ecological, media, historical, sociological, anthropological. In fact these orders or registers were always thrown against the fundamental opposition of the symbolic and semiotic to reveal the destruction of the symbolic order; and to reveal the self-destruction of the semiotic/simulational order (its apparent progression). Whereas Max Weber, whose basic orientation was remarkably similar in general to Baudrillard, opted for responsibility, realism, on the basis of vast historical demonstration, Baudrillard opts for a position beyond responsibility, beyond nihilism, in the play between seduction and simulation, on the basis of vast, implicitly comparative, but above all contemporary demonstration across all domains. Theory becomes a mode of re-enchantment.

Though he often used the genealogical method (see CS: 103ff. and S), this was not a method of constructing progressively more complex forms, or of revealing linear evolutionary trends. It was more a method of defining fundamental cultural divisions, and within these, divisions, shifts and discontinuities in key domains. This method was complemented in *The Transparency of Evil* by the use of social pathology (a more or less abandoned branch of French sociology). The first order of pathology is that of mechanical and dysfunctional breakdown, accident, and so on; the second is that of anomie; the third, that of anomaly, viruses, metastasis. Thus it is Baudrillard, paradoxically, who provided sociology with the most powerful update of Durkheim's theory of social pathology, for Baudrillard's work can be seen as the continuation of Durkheimian sociology in the following perspective: instead of a return to the social norm of liberalism (Mauss, Parsons), society had in fact never been able to return to the equilibrium Durkheim sought and defined as a theoretical norm. For Baudrillard, the liberal democratic consensus and the search for human rights and equality are more dangerous to the symbolic order, more terrorist in practice, than the totalitarian regimes of the 1930s and 1940s. It was this position above all which made Baudrillard's specific variant of millenarianism so difficult to grasp, since he was one of the very few to resist the worship of the Enlightenment project. Instead of celebrating the gradual elimination of superstition by science, modern Western culture induces new radical and self-destructive 'total' superstitions of science (IE: 100). The paradox of the Western drive to perfect control, to the elimination of death, evil and radical otherness, was that this provokes, in the third order, an 'unprecedented pathology': through, on the one hand, the implosion of 'overprotection, over-coding, over-management', and so on (TE: 62); and, on the other, the explosion of liberalisation (TE: 167 and IE: 107ff.). It was as if the complex contrary movement combined both Durkheim's opposite drives beyond all thresholds at the same time: greater totalitarian control (and fatalism) especially of the individual over him/herself on the one side, and deregulation beyond norms (anomie) into the system itself (anomaly) on the other.

It was here, perhaps, that Baudrillard was considered mistaken: this 'unprecedented pathology' does not produce a general breakdown of the social immune system. As with comparable biological processes, the immune system itself is eventually strengthened (perhaps even to an unprecedented level). It is precisely those societies and cultures which come into contact with the higher modes of virulence which are decimated (but this is not unprecedented). Indeed Baudrillard recognised cases, such as that of Japanese society, which played with semiotic culture and technology while still organising itself on other principles (see TE: 143) – a position strangely similar to that of Durkheim on Japan (Durkheim 1982: 118). Baudrillard did not here find his worst-case scenario. Perhaps even he underestimated the way the shift towards extreme phenomena is contained through the process akin to repressive tolerance (suggested by Marcuse). Here again his thought was not at all easy to grasp. Thus he was sometimes accused of racism and sexism because he mocked the human rights movement or the feminist movement. Is he on the far right? His critics did not bother to find out. (Baudrillard's interview on Le Pen is in English, in *New Political Science* 1989: 23–8: 'this is not authentic fascism ... Myth is absent ... just naked virulence, violence exercised in the name of order and in response to the prevailing disorder.') It is within the

Enlightenment project and its attempt at cultural universalisation and homogenisation that racism and sexism make their appearance as modern phenomena – phenomena of the project to eliminate the radical other; 'racism does not come into existence so long as the other remains Other' (IE: 129). Here Baudrillard was consistent: democratic forms are in the process of eliminating the Other 'more surely than by a holocaust' (CMII: 61). Thus we reach a paradoxical conclusion: contemporary fascism is weak, but the present phase of dominant culture (the perfect crime) is even more effectively destructive than virulent fascism.

This was read as Baudrillard's racism and sexism, whereas for Baudrillard it is precisely the terrain of the only effective anti-racism and anti-sexism. It is the reversal of the Enlightenment's perfect crime that is Baudrillard's project: to render the world more mysterious, more enigmatic than he finds it, to restore to the Other the sense of radical alterity. The danger of Baudrillard's position was clear: it could be misread as an outright, not-trivial, reaction. But the logic of his move is implacable: the current terrorism of self-exploitation is worse than any form of pure slavery. 'It is better to be controlled ... oppressed, exploited, persecuted and manipulated by someone other than by oneself' (TE: 167). Virtually all the feminist readers fell immediately into responding that Baudrillard was a proto-fascist chauvinist (Goshorn, in Kellner 1994, is a notable exception). These critiques simply failed to notice Baudrillard's position: that the whole theory of use-value and exchange-value is caught up within the cultural presuppositions of capitalism: for Baudrillard, Marx was not radical enough. (Baudrillard's relation to fascism reveals how radical he was on this point: 'a profound, irrational, demented resistance ... would not have tapped into this massive energy if it hadn't been a resistance to something much worse. Fascism's cruelty, its terror is on the level of this other terror ... ' (SS: 48); and it is worth noting his theses from *Forget Foucault* (FF: 62): 'Fascism's politics is an aesthetics of death, one that already has the look of a nostalgia fad'; and 'everything that has had this look since then must be inspired by fascism' (FF: 62).) As elsewhere, critics launched their derision too soon, and missed their target. The specific difference between Baudrillard's position in symbolic exchange and reactionary 'nostalgia fads' went unnoticed.

Baudrillard's challenge was as much to the mode of theorising as to the substance, and was vulnerable to a number of potential counter-challenges. The most crucial, perhaps, was to the theory of symbolic exchange (a line of criticism of Baudrillard developed by Lyotard). At one level it is simply true that Baudrillard's notion of symbolic exchange, and all the facets of this cultural form which he develops, do not have a basis in work he himself has done as anthropologist or historian: his work is as much a challenge to anthropology as to sociology. His analysis of this form apparently runs counter to all structuralist and functionalist anthropology, and finds its support with marginalised writers such as Bataille and Caillois. Yet things are more complicated than this, since Bataille and Caillois admitted their debt to Mauss's theory of the gift, and Mauss admitted that the framework of his theory remained Durkheimian. It is as if after Mauss the two sides of Durkheimianism, the one examining kinship and cultural structure, the other examining effervescence and symbolic exchange, divided: both repressed their origins in Comte and Durkheim, but retained the millenarian logic (parallel with Marxism) they derived from their common source in Saint-Simon. Thus one could say that however cosmopolitan, global, universal, Baudrillard's range is, he never really escapes the common structure of this theoretical framework, even though he provides a specific variation on it (from Kafka: the apocalypse has happened). The consequences of having adopted this at bottom inescapably evolutionist framework are incalculable, but it is the framework common to Western social science, and thus at this (the most profound) level, Baudrillard is still caught, as was Marx, in a specific cultural formation. Is this still a variation on the sociological law of the three states?

Postmodernism?

Baudrillard has in the last decade been forced by certain commentators into the box marked 'postmodern'. He has rejected this labelling, but not entirely consistently, since occasionally he has been willing to play with the opposition between the modern and the postmodern (see SS: 162–4 and IE: 23, 27, 35, 36, 41, 73, 107, 117). It is quite possible to read Baudrillard in the light of these occasional references and to organise a theory around them. But one suspects readings which follow the ulterior objectives of the reader rather than respecting the concept and the letter of the texts being read. Douglas Kellner led the way here, defining a version of postmodernism, imposing it on Baudrillard, and then claiming that Baudrillard 'exaggerates the break between the modern and the postmodern' (Kellner 1994: 13). Kellner has attempted a critique of Baudrillard that first sets up the modernity–postmodernity model and then claims that Baudrillard underestimates the potential for a Marxist appraisal of this shift and resistance to it. The problem with this line of reading Baudrillard is that it launches the critique too soon at the wrong object: a critique of a phantom based on a crude and dogmatic appeal to a theory of capitalism and of revolutionary mass action and social transformation (see Best (Kellner 1994: 64) and Sawchuck (Ibid. 12)).

My own analysis published in 1991 argued that Baudrillard was not only opposed to postmodernism, his 'whole effort is to combat it' (Gane 1991a: 55). This has been vigorously contested by Kellner ('Gane is completely wrong to claim that Baudrillard's problematic should not be interpreted as being concerned with the postmodern' (Kellner 1994: 14)), and questioned by such recent writers as Ritzer (1997: 76), Smart (1999: 56), and many others. Today Baudrillard's writings are a little more settled on the issue, and it seems evident that he himself has not considered himself in any sense a postmodern theorist. He has used the term rather rarely. If he does have a place for postmodernism, it does not map on to either third or fourth order simulacra categories directly. By locating the emergence of the term in Baudrillard's writing it does look as if its function has been to specify one of the routes not to take within fourth order culture. He has not used it to define the sphere of radical paradox in the modern sciences, where, if any term is used, it is hyper-modernity. It has been used, however, for certain kinds of cultural phenomena such as 'the organic consensus' (IE: 41), the culture of repentance, 'eclectic sentimentality' (IE: 35), 'post-modern intellectual comfort' (IE: 23), and so forth. There has been virtually no resort to the concept in *The Perfect Crime* or *Paroxysm* (P: 48, cf. IE: 107), as if these phenomena were of no interest. In *Fragments: Cool Memories III*, Baudrillard wrote towards the end: 'The Gods have been chased away. Their spectres hover about the deserts of postmodernity. If it took place anywhere, surely the perfect crime had its embodiment here' (FCM: 147). This short passage is framed by passages in German from Hölderlin's poetry to invoke the twilight of the Gods.

Eclecticism?

Through the repertoire available to him from symbolic cultures, Baudrillard adopted a Taoist solution (in SED: 119, PC: 88, IE: 15) or, as in *Fatal Strategies*, the Nietzschean *amor fati*, the active fatalism of be who you are, the rejection of all *ressentiment* and therefore of Christianity and Christian notions of sin and expiation. Critics have considered the possibility that he maliciously watches the world tumble into ruins. But Baudrillard insisted he was merely melancholic, fascinated by the exponential logic of objects in their passionate indifference to human subjectivity. Sometimes it was stoicism. Sometimes it was Manichaeism. Sometimes it was passionate utopianism or pataphysical irony. Each response was suited to its object: dialectical and revolutionary responses were now completely inappropriate modes of resistance. The central characterisation he represented as an active acceptance of the world of catastrophe, catastrophe as naturally marvellous. The real problem was that the language was not consistent and the 'acceptance' of the world often shifted into sheer abuse about the 'stupidity', the 'arrogance', the 'hypocrisy' of the Western humanist elite (for example, IE: 131f.). This contempt for the system that is worse than fascism and the holocaust was often a long way from affirmative weakness (Genosko 1992). Baudrillard's orders of simulation seemed to march through time in blocs: no complexity and overdetermination here, only the secret ironic order of reversibility.

But what was Baudrillard's objective? As it emerges in these texts, it was, as far as sociology and social theory were concerned, to pose one essential question. Is it not a fundamental trap to remain on the terrain of the real, or the revolution to come, or the dialectic, or the world-wide quest for human rights? He certainly might not have been successful; indeed, it is certain that he was not successful, except to reveal in a different mode the vulnerability of the human order. He refused, like Althusser and the Marxists, the route of bourgeois right, of humanism as an ideology, of the Enlightenment project, of technological perfectibility. He refused, like Nietzsche, the 'slave morality' of socialism and feminism as well as all the fashionable forms of despair. He provided theory with a new conception of the Other which avoided essentialism, the sentimentalism of 'the world we have lost', false utopianism and false pessimism. It also evoked a different way of relating to the object and to the Other, a way which refused mastery, truth, accumulation, and proposed illusion, seduction, reversibility. It is tempting to think of this as a proposal for a Taoist or Zen sociology, but Baudrillard guarded against any mystical, soft, flower-power version. The world is ordained by a rigorous order of fate that is objectively brilliant but cruel. One could say that Baudrillard attempted to map out this objective order of things, its immanent logic, its ironic form. Talking of Marx (in *The Illusion of the End*) he said 'the fact that he got the victor wrong in no way detracts from the exactness of Marx's analysis; it merely adds the objective irony which it was lacking' (IE: 51); Orwell's *1984* was actually close to the date of the fall of communism: but again Orwell, like Marx, missed the irony (IE: 41). For Baudrillard, what theory has always found difficult to deal with is not fundamentally the logic of the real, it is precisely the ironic deviation in the real. This is why theory is naive. The problem here is that Baudrillard did not seem to find the way forward: his efforts in the Gulf War episode were in their own way perhaps a genre of naivety in the symbolic. He more or less appeared to admit this himself: the 'surreptitious intervention on the side of the void ... fell into the same black hole, the same virtual space, as the non-events of which it was to speak ... An apparently irresolvable paradox. But the idea is not dead' (IE: 16). An intervention, and from outside the virtual. But vulnerable.

CHAPTER 4

Reality and Hyperreality

> We are beyond the Last Judgement, in immortality ... And it is there indeed that hell begins, the hell of the unconditional realisation of all ideas, the hell of the real ... (PC: 102)

There are many ideas and concepts that have made Baudrillard famous. Three linked theses have given his writing a certain notoriety and have become particularly infamous. The first is that *only* the cultures of the West have developed a category, a notion and an ideology of the real and have produced, and reproduced, a real world. There is no universal process of the social construction of reality. The second is that in its subsequent evolution, Western culture introduced significant modifications to the way it produced the real, by intensifying it and heightening it into a domain of reality in hyperspace: hyperreality. The third is the thesis that the long-term logic of Western culture also leads to the problematisation of the category of the real, both by absorbing it into the virtual and by shattering it into fractal dimensions. Some of these propositions were already outlined as a possibility in the work of Nietzsche. Nietzsche's version, however, was polarised towards the philosophical tradition and the genealogy of the concept of the real within it, from Plato to Kant. Baudrillard does not locate his analysis of the real within philosophical discourse, but follows it through all the major dimensions of Western culture. This chapter examines these three highly contested theses. It will take Baudrillard's own view to be that the concept of reality remains an order of illusion, but one of a uniquely abject type. It is not therefore a question, at least for Baudrillard, of fictional orders against factual ones, but more paradoxically of two quite different kinds of illusion.

The symbolic order

In *Symbolic Exchange and Death* Baudrillard attempted to outline his thesis that in societies where symbolic exchange is the dominant principle, cultures do not relate to the 'reality' of the world but to the world and cosmos in narrative, fable, as radical illusion. Against the view developed by the European Enlightenment that these fables are based on ignorance and superstition, Baudrillard argues that they are subtle, and indeed continue to be vital for human existence. The doctrines emanating from the paradigm of the real are secondary, and generally perhaps in the end disastrous for human existence, or at least it would be an impossible, nightmarish world if they should ever overwhelm entire cultures, drawing them into the 'hell of the real' (PC: 102).

If as a first step it is important to note that Baudrillard's analysis takes up theses from Marcel Mauss (on the gift), Georges Bataille (on the accursed share), Ferdinand de Saussure (on the anagram), Freud (on totemism), it is clear that Baudrillard's ideas cannot be restricted to these resources, and his relation to them is critical and selective. On the one hand, he was the translator from German into French of Muhlmann's work on revolutionary millenarianism. His work draws on a range of anthropological writing beyond Mauss; for example, Leenhardt, Jaulin, the Ortigues, Malinowski and others (as recently examined by Genosko (1998: 25–47)). On the other hand, Baudrillard's position is developed against and contests theses developed by Levi-Strauss and Lacan, as well as Marxist anthropologists like Claude Meillasoux. Baudrillard's ideas are reconstructed then in an analysis which over time becomes aligned with Nietzsche's critique of cultures of *ressentiment*. He aimed to radicalise these central propositions by limiting the applicability of the ideas of Marx and Freud, and reorganising theses from Nietzsche, Saussure and Lacan.

In *Symbolic Exchange and Death*, only the final two chapters (on death, and on the anagram) aim to develop a theory of symbolic exchange itself; the first four chapters deal with production, simulacra, fashion, and the body in semiotic cultures where the real has already become important. Indeed, even in the chapter on death (Chapter 5) only a subsection actually deals with death in primitive cultures. What interests Baudrillard is to think of death as a form, as the crucial figure of reversibility. Baudrillard's orientation in the analysis is clear from the start: primitive peoples 'have no biological concept of death' (SED: 131); he distances himself from Western notions which converge 'on the illusion of a biological materiality of death' (SED: 131) for his thesis is that the material illusion of death is itself only a derived simulacrum. Death as a form in primitive cultures is here (1976) explained in the anthropological paradigm as a type of 'relation' – more specifically as ' ... a circulation of gifts and counter-gifts', one 'as intense as the circulation of precious goods and women' (SED: 131). Baudrillard's anthropology is based then on classical exchange theory as a theory of social determination: such exchanges fall 'under the jurisdiction of the group'. This is also true of all processes whereby social beings enter into the symbolic order through rituals of initiation which are always processes of exchange: 'young initiates circulate amongst the living adults and the dead ancestors: they are given and returned, whereby they accede to symbolic recognition' (SED: 134). It is also true of the fundamental exchange of women between groups, produced by the incest taboo.

The social analysis is framed explicitly within Mauss's theory of the social nature of the gift. But what makes this theory into a new radical anthropology is its critical appropriation of Lacan, that is the symbolic is conceived as 'a social relation which puts an end to the real ... and puts an end to the opposition between the real and the imaginary' (SED: 133). Baudrillard's intervention here rejects all attempts to analyse primitive cultures as if they had the same (triadic) structures as modern European cultures. Thus while the terminology puts the discussion firmly on the ground of Lacanian theory, it introduces a critical variation: the real (and reality principle) is not a primary or a fundamental term.[1] The category of the real becomes problematic, it is what remains from a disjunction of the two basic terms life and death: 'the reality principle is never anything other than the imaginary of the other term' (SED: 133). Baudrillard announces his own conclusions rather dogmatically: the symbolic debt is the basis of all possible culture (SED: 134). In place of the idea of universal structures of the unconscious as developed in Freudian theory, Baudrillard suggests that the specifically Freudian processes of repression and the unconscious come into existence only with those modern cultures which destroy the collective nature of symbolic exchange:

> The unconscious is social in the sense that it is made up of all that could not be exchanged socially or symbolically. And so it is with death: it is exchanged in any case, and, at best, it will be exchanged in accordance with a social ritual, as with the primitives; at worst it will be 'redeemed' by an individual labour of mourning. (SED: 134)

Thus there is here a basic set of social principles which specify social processes where the symbolic is dominant. The first is that the incest taboo 'lies at the basis of alliances amongst the living'. The second holds that ritual 'initiation lies at the basis of alliances amongst the living and the dead' (SED: 134). The third principle develops in relation to a theory of primitive cultures in which there is a specific kind of relationship between agency and its alters: its double, spirit or shadow. These three principles form the basic propositions of Baudrillard's anthropology, and they are derived directly from Durkheim and Mauss. It is important to note here that Baudrillard in this work outlines a notion of impossible exchange that is not identical with that which forms the object of the later book called *L'Échange impossible* (1999).

But Baudrillard immediately draws some very radical conclusions. His first and basic observation is that the soul as double found in the symbolic order is quite different from the soul within Christianity. With the primitive other, there is a partnership between agent and its double. This is not a relation of either mirror image or alienated subject. Following Nietzsche closely, Baudrillard argues that alienation only arises with the formation of the image of the other as an abstract and irreconcilable agency: 'alienation begins with the internalisation of the Master by the emancipated slave: there is no alienation as long as the duel-relation of the master and the slave lasts' (SED: 141). Thus the third fundamental anthropological principle discussed here suggests that primitive cultures situate agency within a structure of duel/dual relations with their others. These agents converse with, confront, play with this shadow in a pact that is lodged within a system of exchanges.

Baudrillard's relation to Bataille is highly significant, for although Baudrillard is highly critical of Bataille, his argument is that Bataille offers a 'premonition' of a solution to these issues raised by Mauss and Durkheim, Marx and Nietzsche (SED: 158). The anthropological paradigm now becomes clear. The central ideas are still articulated around the exchange between groups, and symbolic exchange is defined as a 'social relation' governed by symbolic debt. The conceptualisation adopts terms such as ritual, reversibility, gift and counter-gift, sacrifice, excess, accursed share, expenditure and paroxysm (SED: 155–8). The temporal cycles of return predominate. It is a paradigm which has no place for the concept of fetishism, which the Durkheim–Mauss school had radically abandoned after Comte had brought it into ridicule. It is by reference to this anthropological paradigm and its Lacanian modification that Baudrillard was able to indicate a general theory of the emergence of the real and the reality principle. The real then enters as that which does not partake of the cycle of symbolic exchange and presents as a remainder a dangerous threat to the ritualised social.

Seduction

Baudrillard evidently provides a basic set of theoretical terms to demarcate the symbolic from the semiotic cultures, and thus a way of thinking about the symbolic as opposed to the semiotic. The key terms are presented and discussed in various contexts in his work but essentially revolve around the idea that with seduction as a symbolic instance there can be no representation, 'because in seduction the distance between the real and its double, and the distortion between the Same and the Other, is abolished' (S: 67). The various attempts to develop the theory of seduction and the symbolic are probably Baudrillard's most ambitious projects. The symbolic order is not a culture in depth, with base and superstructure, nor does it have manifest and latent levels of determination and overdetermination: there is no abyss into profound meaning, with multiple layers of hidden dimensions. There is, according to Baudrillard, only what he calls the 'superficial abyss' of appearance. One example he provides is the Narcissus myth: the mirror is not one which provides Narcissus with an ideal of himself. The 'mirror of water is not a surface of reflection, but of absorption' (S: 67).

Baudrillard's central example, which is repeated throughout his subsequent works, is the difference between the anagram and the sign, at least as these terms were developed within the thought of Saussure (and outlined in *Symbolic Exchange and Death*). Many of Baudrillard's own conceptual images for the order of seduction are framed so that they do not imply depth, a favourite being the image of the watermark, another the palindrome. Depth, on the other hand, is structured into Saussure's triadic conception of signifier, signified and referent. For Baudrillard this conception quite coherently reflects a cultural form in which there already exists a formal separation between (conceptual) images and discrete objects (their referents). In cultures where symbolic orders articulate the appearances of the world through mythic narrative, no such separations can exist. Or, more precisely, one should say that what is represented is an order of things quite different from the order of objects which make up the 'real' in the Western system of 'referents'.

The real

In his development of these ideas in his subsequent work, another Nietzschean term becomes central as Baudrillard reconstructs entirely his notion of the social and social relations at the end of the 1970s. This term is radical illusion. In his essay *Seduction*, Baudrillard discusses the aesthetic dimension of seduction and illustrates his conception of the genealogy of simulacra with reference to art. The Renaissance break with medieval forms is most strikingly seen, he suggests, in the theory and adoption of perspective, vanishing points, and a new geometry of representation. Instead of concentrating on this side of representation (the gaze on to the real world), Baudrillard's interest is in the 'enchanted' simulacral form: the *trompe l'oeil*. *Trompe l'oeil* plays on Renaissance rationalised perspectivism as surrealism later plays on twentieth-century functionalism. In both cases the enchanted form plays with the rational order, reveals reality to be nothing other than a principle, that is 'a simulacrum which the experimental hypersimulation of the *trompe l'oeil* undermines' (S: 63). Baudrillard's analysis suggests that *trompe l'oeil* reverses 'the privileged position of the gaze. The eye, instead of generating a space that spreads out, is but the internal vanishing point for a convergence of objects' (S: 63).

In order to recover Baudrillard's analysis of the irruption of the real, it is necessary then to reverse his analysis of the form of the *trompe l'oeil*, the disenchanted form produced by rational perspective: profane horizon, vanishing point, the modern gaze. It is a gaze which is master, seizes and possesses its field in depth and the objects within it (cf. Foucault on *Las Meninas* (1970: 3–16)). Baudrillard suggests that here there is a relationship between two simulacra, a relationship which is quite different from that of the primitive soul and its double. The enchanted, *trompe l'oeil* form plays with and reveals the structures of reality by invoking a veritable 'hyperpresence of things' (S: 63). Thus emerges the 'uncanniness of the *trompe l'oeil*' – the strange light it casts on this entirely new, Western reality which emerged triumphant with the Renaissance. The *trompe l'oeil* is 'the ironic simulacrum of that reality' (S: 64). At the heart of the Renaissance then – and Baudrillard discusses its ramifications in political and theological terms – is the secret of a new power revealed in mastery over the play of reversion of structures, its 'blind spot', just as 'the great Jesuits and theologians all knew that God did not exist; this was their secret, and the secret of their strength' (S: 66). Modern power is manipulative cynical power.

Baudrillard's conceptualisation gives the thesis of the emergence of the real an historical and epistemological contextualisation: the real is equivalent to the rational, the true, and therefore is simply a new type of fiction, the disenchanted form which comes with a project of disillusionment. Certainly a number of nineteenth-century anthropologists such as Comte and Spencer found it difficult to believe that primitives could live in relation to the world as a mythical whole. But it soon became accepted among anthropologists that this did not prevent any primitive society from relating to the phenomena of their environments. These societies integrated into a world through fabulous narrative. For Baudrillard, the real is never privileged as reflecting an exterior truth into culture. It can only become a category within a culture when the symbolic order has lost its pre-eminent place. Baudrillard's thesis is that these cultures are comparatively speaking very late developments in human history and he locates them in an analysis from the reformation, and more generally the period of the Renaissance in Western Europe. With the Renaissance there is a sharp transition away from the notion of enlightenment as wisdom, to enlightenment as discovery of new realities, and this induces a radical disenchantment of the world of illusions – an avenue which was systematically prepared in the West by Christianity itself in its long struggles against the symbolic communities and their millenarian cults.[2]

What intrigues Baudrillard throughout this analysis are the wrong types of response to the challenges of European culture. First, the particular forms taken by the Counter-Reformation, and the attempts within Christianity to rebuff and check the Enlightenment (through 'efficient simulacra, such as the organisation's apparatus, as well as bureaucratic, theatrical ... training and educational machinery which aims, for the first time in a systematic fashion, to fashion an ideal nature on the model of the child' (SED: 52). And secondly, movements against the industrial revolution, and the tragic fate of the revolution in the increasingly bureaucratised edifice of communism with its celebration of the proletarian as ideal man. The Jesuits did not believe in God, and Communist Party hierarchies did not believe in communism. Today the political hierarchies do not believe in democracy. It is cynical power that is effective.

But the era of the real and its ideological mystification was only a relatively brief episode in Western cultural history. Baudrillard's analysis here is still sociological and semiotic. His sociology is concerned to register the emergence of a new situation brought about by the failure of the project of the dialectical transcendence of capitalism. At some time between 1968 and 1973 Baudrillard abandoned the hope of social revolution on the model of 1789 or 1917, and abandoned the Marxist framework of political economy, and class struggle in events of historical scope. He had already worked out a significant variation within the Marxist paradigm of the evolution of consumer society but this was still framed within a notion of capitalist production as ultimately determinant. But with *The Mirror of Production* he also added that with the evolution of capitalism itself towards monopoly forms, capitalism was no longer the system theorised by Marx. He argues that the (economic) mode of production is no longer distinct from superstructures. When this separation disappears within monopoly capitalism itself, the cultural code becomes hegemonic and the category of a completely separate reality – as well as the principle of representation – is weakened. Baudrillard moves from Marx to Nietzsche as a more prescient thinker, and argues that there subsequently ensues a crisis in the culture which comes to affect all levels: science, art, technology, politics. A series of boundary crises emerges, for example between subject and object, and even between subject and subject. These crises emerge in conditions where, paradoxically, there occur both a revolutionary liberation of energy (and reversal of gravity field) and, at the same time, a loss of the referential and dialectical frame which acted as container of the previous system.

Hyperreality

The 'golden age of alienation' is over and Western cultures enter a new configuration with the arrival of simulation processes – the 'ecstasy of communication'. There is a brief period when Baudrillard calls the effect of simulation the 'neo-real': the effect of cybernetic and operational sciences, and the models they establish, is that 'reality itself is abolished, obliterated, in favour of this neo-reality of the model' (CS: 126). But taking up the term hyperreality from a movement in modern art, Baudrillard identified the dissolution of relations between subject and object, real and fake, true and false, in the triumph of consumer capitalism (mass affluence and the fashion cycle, and the hegemony of mass media – particularly television). Taken together, these new forces modify political and cultural events so fundamentally that in effect they no longer exist apart from the mode of their representation, just as the new modes of investigation in the social sciences or the natural sciences are independent of their objects. Across the cultural spectrum the spectacular increase in the capacities to construct and to invent the world reverses all theoretical pre-suppositions.

Thus with hyperreality comes the collapse of the 'society of the spectacle' and society as dramaturgy. What is henceforth privileged is the 'meticulous reduplication of the real, preferably through another reproductive medium such as advertising or photography' (SED: 71). This shift is defined by Baudrillard in the first instance as a the 'ecstasy of denegation' or the effacement of the 'contradiction of the real and the imaginary' (SED: 72). A key precursor of this movement he argues was the *nouveau roman*, which tried to produce a 'pure objectivity ... a meticulous but blind reality', and this puts an end to perspectival depth and relief. The basic aim of this aesthetic 'project is to construct a void round the real' (SED: 72). In theory, Baudrillard argues, there are always a number of possible 'modalities' of simulation: the immediate close up 'reading' of the object; splitting the object and reduplicating it serially; the serial form (cf. Warhol); and the basic form itself, the binary code and digitality. Thus hyperrealist painting is not theoretically the essence of this form: it is but its flawed ironic duplication, since there is still the artist's signature and the 'border that separates' the painted surface of the work of art and the wall of the gallery. Baudrillard defines the real as 'that of which it is possible to provide an equivalent reproduction', but only then marks the emergence of the hyperreal as that which precedes the real, or more specifically a real which is 'always already reproduced' (SED: 73).

Baudrillard's analysis then does not, at least here (*Symbolic Exchange and Death*), suggest that the real is annihilated, or disposed of, in a dramatic expulsion, but that 'reality ... is entirely impregnated by an aesthetic ... has become inseparable from its own image' (SED: 75). The question at this point is posed very directly: 'Are we at the end of the real?' Baudrillard's answer is 'No ... the barriers of representation rotate crazily, an implosive madness ... today reality itself is hyperrealist' (SED: 74–5). Thus, at least in theory, what happens in this shift is a kind of fusion of real and imaginary, so that there is no longer a play of representation based on clearly demarcated separations: the real 'swallows' its alienated double and paradoxically becomes, at the same time, transparent to itself. In this fusion, the aesthetic dimension enters into 'reality', even into what he calls the new aesthetic 'game of reality' (SED: 74). This is no longer external repression, but the installation of powerful new inner 'controls'. The reality principle passes, the more intimate simulation principle takes its place (SED: 75–6).

It should be pointed out of course that these propositions were developed in the mid-1970s, and were expressly aimed at capturing a vision of a society in which the 'information' revolution was becoming active. Baudrillard thus was among the first to indicate the significance of credit cards, computers, networking, virtualisation, as these became significant for the first time as a mass phenomenon of affluent societies (see Ritzer's Introduction in CS: 1–24). His theoretical position at this time was also complemented by a number of striking cultural and political examples. One of the most famous was his analysis of Disneyland, rounded out and developed substantially in his eponymous essay on (hyperreal) America (and elsewhere), in which he argued that American modernity itself was paradigmatically developed as third-order simulacra. Disneyland is part of and not distinct from the reality of America, or, equivalently, America is part of the hyperreal modernity of Disneyland.

But even as early as the 1970s Baudrillard outlined a thesis which has been far more notorious: even the Vietnam War was a simulated war. He was careful to point out here that 'war is no less atrocious for being only a simulacrum – the flesh suffers just the same' (SS: 37). But even so, what he had begun to argue was that something fundamental had changed in the world order. This has rarely been picked up in commentaries on Baudrillard. His argument was that a decisive shift in the world system had occurred at the moment China entered into the play of 'peaceful co-existence' with the USA during the Vietnam conflict. His argument is that:

> China's apprenticeship to a global *modus vivendi*, the shift from a global strategy of revolution to one of shared forces and empires, the transition from a radical alternative to political alternation in a system now essentially regulated ... this is what was at stake in the war in Vietnam ... behind this simulacrum of fighting to the death and of ruthless global stakes, the two adversaries are fundamentally in solidarity against something else, unnamed, never spoken ... Tribal, communitarian, pre-capitalist structures, every form of exchange, of language, of symbolic organisation, that is what must be abolished, that is the object of murder in war – and war itself ... (SS: 37)

There is then within Baudrillard's analytic scheme the opposition between the semiotic and symbolic cultures, and in a sense this comes to operate as a referent for his analysis: the violence of the Western cultures and their political and military powers is aimed, through the very simulacra of modern war (that is with simulated adversaries), towards the destruction of all 'radical alternatives' to the semiotic cultures, which are the true casualties of these events.

Extremes

In the third order the code or matrix is determinant in a system in which sign-value is the predominant form of the law of value. In this phase there is, then, a fusion of the real into simulation: the hyperreal. Just what the specific chronological phases of these developments have been in various cultures is not charted, but it is clear that the stage of the code (whether as American modernity, monopoly capitalism, and so on), has, at least as Baudrillard's theory suggests, been eclipsed by a new stage of the 'real' – the hyperreal. With sign-value and the code (the third order) there was still the operation of the system of values in hyperreal culture, there was still the possibility of a kind of exchange: 'hyperrealism is the apex of both art and the real, by means of the privileges and prejudices that found them' (SED: 73). But in the new fourth-order situation there emerges only the 'law of the confusion of categories' (TE: 9). Here the process of the liberation of energies reaches a new point, a 'tendency for systems to explode beyond their own limits ... in the sense of an increase in their power, a fantastic potentialisation whereby their own very existence is put at risk' (TE: 5). The consequence of such radical liberalisation of energy is that things are thus subject not just to indeterminacy, they become subject to the uncertainty principle (TE: 4).

   This new situation is charted as a series of consequences of the forces unleashed in earlier phases. In the second order there was a clear separation of the real and the imaginary, in the third the real is contained in the space of simulation (the imaginary is expelled), and so the real still carries the given weight of its inherited formal constitution. But as the rule of the precession of simulacra begins to have consequences for the system in which it evolved, the effects are felt in the first instance in the irruption of transpolitical forms. Baudrillard's first book of the 1990s, *The Transparency of Evil: Essays in Extreme Phenomena*, begins by examining transaesthetic, transsexual, and transeconomic phenomena. If in the first instance the effect of the semiotic is to break down each sphere, each species, each body into elements, so that their combinations can be known, eventually the transference of elements beyond the sphere to which they originally belonged occurs. Once this begins to happen on an extended scale the very lines dividing the spheres begin to dissolve and the elements no longer have a definite place in the world. So the transition from the third to the fourth order of simulacra appears to occur in two steps. The first is the immediate impact of transpolitical phenomena, where the break with the 'natural' location of the element is intensely felt. But the second step leads beyond this into the real indifference of combinations outside of any combinatory system or matrix. When this latter stage is reached not only is there a radical indetermination at the level of the simulated and the real, but also all the previously secure categories of social knowledge which have guaranteed the articulated spheres of being are undermined: economic, political, religious, sexual, cultural, as well as the human itself.

   Baudrillard's position here is itself a little ambivalent. 'At the fourth, the fractal (or viral, or radiant) stage of value, there is no point of reference at all, and value radiates in all directions, occupying all interstices, without reference to anything whatsoever, by virtue of contiguity. At the fractal stage there is at no point any equivalence, whether natural or general. Properly speaking there is now no law of value ... ' (TE: 5). The new situation is not characterised by any sort of play between the real, simulation and the imaginary, but by processes of replication, reduplication, metastasis. And when these extreme phenomena encounter one another as aleatoric contiguities, is it possible to say unambiguously what is happening? Not according to Baudrillard, because, as with the case of microphysics, 'it is as impossible to make estimations between beautiful and ugly, true and false, or good and evil, as it is simultaneously to calculate a particle's speed and position' (TE: 5–6).

These observations are enough to suggest that the phenomena Baudrillard identifies in his precession of simulacra are not to be taken as steps in a single and simple process of increasing technical sophistication: the emergence of fourth-order simulacra is above all paradoxical, since in an unprecedented mode, two things (one in the real, the other in the hyperreal) occur simultaneously. Baudrillard is famous for his thesis that Western cultures, having produced the real, are in the process of virtualising it. But another thesis is also maintained: that Western cultures cannot stop the process of producing more and more of the 'real' within the orders of simulation themselves. This is expressed explicitly: 'reality is at its height ... what we must do is think this unconditional realization of the world, which is at the same time its unconditional simulacrum' (PC: 64–5). What this means in political terms is that the drive to a new world order is effectively a process of the annihilation of all other cultural formations, which takes place, not openly as a direct and immediate objective, but within the encounter of simulacral forms of war and politics, where the intervention of new media heightens at the same time the reality and the undecidability of all events.

But within the Western cultures themselves there is also uncertainty about what the real is, so on the one hand the real is a refuge, and is indeed still the dominant simulacral form (PC: 64); on the other hand, no one believes that their lives can be reduced to a formula of the reality principle (PC: 96):

> The point is not, then, to assert that the real does or does not exist – a ludicrous proposition which well expresses what that reality means to us: a tautological hallucination ('the real exists, I have met it'). There is merely a movement of the exacerbation of reality towards paroxysm, where it involutes of its own accord and implodes leaving no trace, not even the sign of its end. (PC: 46)

The play in this logic, and the possibilities it opens up, cannot, however, be grasped by critical theory appropriate to the analysis of a set of dialectical potentialities entailing unquestioned real historical events. The system of Western cultural logics is in principle now quite different. Fourth-order simulacral space and time are no longer framed within the schema of the reality principle. Baudrillard presents this as a revolutionary reversal in the following way: the conventional reality principle

> is based on distinction between things, yet on their correlation within a single space – their presence one to another. The schema of physics, by contrast, is based on their inseparability, yet on the absence of things from one another (they do not interact in a homogeneous space). (PC: 54)

It is now becoming much clearer that Baudrillard's analysis is not at all one which attempts to follow the fusion of the real and simulacra, subject and its object, 'their magical confusion in so-called irrational thought', but tries to grasp the fact that the 'objective illusion is the impossibility of an objective truth once the subject and object are no longer distinct, and the impossibility of any knowledge based on that distinction' (PC: 54). Far from being passive in this new situation Baudrillard takes up a very specific and complex (even extreme position) (PC: 56): he locates those forms which subvert the process of the unconditional hyperrealisation of the world. Thus there is a kind of strategic alignment: on the one hand, the resistance by the cultures which offer continued symbolic resistance to the new cultural order (the remaining tribal peoples, for example); but on the other, the identification at the edge of Western cultures of those moments and forms of poetic reversion, and those increasingly eccentric singularities, which have not been and cannot be integrated and subordinated to hyperrealisation. This radical thought must be three quite contradictory things at the same time: the power of radical illusion; imminent in the real as a material illusion; but also eccentric to the real (PC: 96).

CHAPTER 5

Uncertainty

> The aim of science and technology would seem
> to be that of presenting us with a definitively
> unreal world, beyond all criteria of truth and reality.
> The revolution of our time is the uncertainty
> revolution. (TE: 42–3)

In their book *Intellectual Impostures* Alan Sokal and Jean Bricmont attack Baudrillard amongst others for shamelessly abusing scientific knowledge (Sokal & Bricmont 1998: 137–43). This chapter examines their critique.

The attack

They begin their attack on Baudrillard by pointing out that some of his use of scientific language is metaphorical, or what they call the 'use of technical ... notions out of context' (Ibid. 137). Their example is Baudrillard's description of the Gulf War as no longer having taken place in Euclidean space, but in 'hyperspace with multiple refractivity' (Ibid. 139). They admit they do not understand this but grant that the use is metaphorical and so not an abuse, just 'a Baudrillardian invention'.

But, they say, Baudrillard abuses science when his examples are not metaphorical. They cite a long passage from *Fatal Strategies*, which they admit is 'difficult' to understand but seems clearly to be wrong. Baudrillard says 'what science senses now, at the physical and biological limits of its exercise, is that there is not only ... uncertainty, but a possible reversibility of physical laws'. Sokal and Bricmont remark that reversibility means 'invariance with respect to time inversion' and if this is what Baudrillard means it is already part of the Newtonian world. It is 'non-reversibility' which is new, only discovered in 1964 and relates to as yet not fully understood processes of 'weak interactions' (Ibid. 139).

They move on to another long citation of some eight paragraphs, from *The Illusion of the End* (IE: 110–14), where Baudrillard talks about chaos theory, cause and effect, and apparently embraces a 'high density of scientific and pseudo-scientific terminology – inserted in sentences that are, as far as we can make out, devoid of meaning' (Sokal & Bricmont 1998: 142). But at least they do contain references to defined scientific ideas whereas 'more often' Baudrillard produces only the pompous and the meaningless, the following being their chosen example:

> There is no better model of the way in which the computer screen and the mental screen of our brain are interwoven than Moebius's topology, with its peculiar contiguity of near and far, inside and outside, object and subject within the same spiral. It is in accordance with this same model that information and communication are constantly turning round upon themselves in an incestuous circumvolution, a superficial conflation of subject and object, within and without, question and answer, event and image, and so on. The form is inevitably that of a twisted ring reminiscent of the mathematical symbol for infinity. (TE: 56)

Sokal and Bricmont change their tone slightly as they sum up by saying now that whether as metaphor or not (they really have to take this line in the light of the last sentence of Baudrillard they cite) the function of these formulations is to 'give an impression of profundity to trite observations about sociology or history ... one wonders what would be left of Baudrillard's thought if the verbal veneer covering it were stripped away' (Sokal & Bricmont 1998: 143). So Sokal and Bricmont are not too careful to distinguish between metaphorical and non-metaphorical use of language. What they suggest happens in Baudrillard's case is that 'scientific terminology is mixed up with a non-scientific vocabulary that is employed with equal sloppiness' (Ibid.). They have only asserted this, for on careful inspection they try simply to let Baudrillard appear self-evidently incredible.

They do not attempt any reconstruction of Baudrillard's ideas or analyses, but just 'wonder' what it might be beneath the 'verbal veneer'. But if they have not reconstructed the problematic how can they reach any judgment as to whether he introduces metaphors 'in a context where they are manifestly irrelevant' and in 'total disregard for their meaning' (Ibid.)? The first piece of advice Sokal and Bricmont give to such theorists is 'It's a good idea to know what one is talking about' (Ibid. 176). But even this is not really the point, for only a project which is extremely short of seriousness could think that Baudrillard might be a theoretical physicist, or might be capable of offering anything to theoretical physics other than a poetic insight. But if this is understood, then to read Baudrillard as a poet having resource to the language of physics means reading quite a different project. Curiously, Sokal and Bricmont start their chapter noting that 'Baudrillard is well known for his reflections on the problems of reality, appearance and illusion' (Ibid. 137), but when it comes to the analysis they do not seem to know or indeed want to know the first thing about these reflections or a poetics of scientific language.

Chaos

At first sight Baudrillard's recent writings make use of terminology from across the sciences, from mathematics (non-Euclidean space, chaos, fractals), astronomy and physics (black hole, implosion, singularity), through biology (DNA, genome, genetic engineering), in a way that has, as Sokal and Bricmont (Ibid. 125–36) show, become focused around the idea of 'postmodern' science (that is that there has been a revolution in the sciences across the board, comparable to the shift from Newton to Einstein). And such recourse to imagery from the sciences is nothing new, for it was central to that tradition in social theory that tried to establish a social science, from Marx and Engels to Althusser, from Comte to Baudrillard. For Baudrillard there has been a shift: 'Marx was always in the "orthodoxy" of things and not in the chaos of things' (BL: 206). He could well have said Comte or Engels, or Durkheim. What is evident about the writers Sokal and Bricmont discuss, particularly Baudrillard, Lyotard and Deleuze, is that they have consciously attempted in very different ways, to get into the chaos of things, courting notoriety as they have done so.

For Baudrillard at any rate, getting into 'chaos' turned out to be a vast enterprise. Sokal and Bricmont take great delight in mocking Baudrillard's observation that science creates paradoxes such as the possibility of a reversal of cause and effect: 'even in human affairs, we seriously doubt that an action in the present could affect an event in the past!' (Sokal & Bricmont 1998: 140–1; note at this point Baudrillard's very careful language 'put in mind of', etc.). Cause and effect are no longer unquestionably linear for Baudrillard, and indeed they were not for Althusser who argued this had already been problematised in Spinoza (structural causality). In fiction theory, such as that of Borges, the theme of retrospective causality is treated as a delightful paradox. But if we use Althusser's types of cause, mechanical, expressive and structural, it seems Althusser himself tried to 'enter into the chaos of things' in his very last period with greater and greater emphasis on chance, aleatoric encounters, paradoxical conjunctures (Elliott 1998). Certainly there are a number of exemplary essays on the problem of how, in human affairs, actions in the present can affect events in the past once one accepts that the past and present are not separable (for example, 'Kafka and his Precursors' in Borges 1970: 234–6).

But what is meant by fractals, by Euclidean space, or rather non-Euclidean space? Here Sokal and Bricmont suggest that non-Euclidean geometries hold that 'there can be either an infinite number of parallel lines or else none at all' (Sokal & Bricmont 1998: 138). Fractal objects 'are more complicated (than ordinary objects), and need to be assigned several distinct "dimensions" to describe different aspects of their geometry ... the "Hausdorff dimension" of a fractal object is in general not a whole number' (Ibid. 127). These definitions seem remarkably vague. There are very many popular accounts of postmodern science which give detailed definitions of these and similar developments in the sciences (such as Coles 1998), let alone the now widely available introductions to fractals by Mandelbrot and others, and to the postmodern universe of Hawkins. What is at issue (as Sokal and Bricmont grasp well) is whether or not there has been a fundamental shift in the sciences from a conception of an ordered and progressive universe (one might say like a world of well-ordered human affairs) to one which is altogether more strange and paradoxical (like a chaos of human affairs).

Revolution

The theme that runs through the account by Sokal and Bricmont is the thesis that the examples and concepts picked up by Baudrillard and Lyotard and others are in the main only 'new tools ... but in no way call into question traditional scientific epistemology' (Sokal & Bricmont 1998: 127). This begs the question as to what counts as a scientific epistemology, since what is at issue is whether there has been a shift (whether one calls it epistemological in the strong sense or not) within the sciences themselves towards a point at which the question 'does God play dice?' becomes meaningful. Baudrillard, who after all is interested in the cultural logic of these forms, takes an extreme position: the revolution in the sciences is part of and can even be taken as emblematic of a total socio-cultural transition in Western societies, one affecting all levels and all processes. His proposition is that this shift is not a problem of fuzzy boundaries, but an immanent revolution affecting core institutions and values (if these still exist).

In order to understand Baudrillard's position then, it is necessary to reconstruct and define the use and meaning of the concepts he adopts to make an account of this transition. It seems irrelevant to ask whether Baudrillard has actually understood the nature of a theorem of subatomic physics. Since he is probably working from texts of scientific popularisation the question should be addressed elsewhere. The question is more interesting if posed first in terms of the significance he wants to give these terms and examples as an account of shifts in contemporary culture, and secondly in terms of a challenge to conventional theories and accounts of them: so as to learn something of what Baudrillard might have contributed not to theoretical physics but to theoretical sociology.

Sokal and Bricmont start where they are strong: as professional physicists they ought to be capable of correcting a misunderstanding of a technical formula. But if we reverse this and start where Baudrillard is strong, we start with the analysis of contemporary Western consumerism, fashion, media, new information technologies and cultural virtualisation. Baudrillard wants to argue that consumerism which was in its high form a system of the exchange and consumption of objects (for which he delivered a classic definition), has become a different phenomenon as a consequence of a massive increase in energy inputs, deregulation, the information revolution, globalisation. Here Baudrillard is perfectly circular: the experience of this phenomenon is expressed as fragmentary (*Cool Memories*); the strange forms emerging in the advanced sciences are raided for imagery which will evoke a reversal of a cultural gravitational field, so that the very familiar dimensions of the world are broken up – just as they are 'broken up' the term 'fractal' becomes available. Just at the moment reality itself is increasingly problematic as a term, the idea of virtual reality becomes available. Curiously the retrospective analysis of the Columbine massacre on British television includes a clip from the film *The Matrix* (a film in which Baudrillard's own book *Simulacra and Simulation* appears at a crucial point) to reveal how the media reports were influenced not by what 'actually happened' but by ideas emanating from mass culture itself (including in this case Baudrillard's own theory of it).

But let us start an examination of these thematic terms. The first – and this is picked up by Sokal and Bricmont – is that of the transition of space-time from Euclidean, to non-Euclidean space (or to hyperspace), as they cite Baudrillard's essay on the Gulf War: ' ... the apocalypse of real time and pure war along with the triumph of the virtual over the real, are realised at the same time, in the same space-time ... It is a sign that the space of the event has become a hyperspace with multiple refractivity'(Sokal & Bricmont 1998: 137). Baudrillard used these terms earlier (in 1976) in discussing opinion polls, and asked: 'do they yield exact photographs of reality ... or a refraction of this reality in a hyperspace of simulation whose curvature we do not even know?' (SED: 66). Opinion polls as refraction in hyperspace. Here Baudrillard makes it clear we are dealing with statistics, probabilities and operational cybernetics. What the introduction of the term hyperspace does here is to bring to the rather banal shift from election to opinion polling an exaggeration equivalent to the non-banal shift in passing from walking to travelling at the speed of light. Without a definition, hyperspace must be understood from the example and context: above all it marks out a space where things have a logic which is strangely different, that is not a simple extension (from walking to running). The term refraction in hyperspace also functions differently from any term used to describe people walking to vote. As well as indicating a qualitative shift it is reproduced in theory. It would be possible to say of the expression that it is 'a fabulous fiction whose index of refraction in (true or false) reality is zero' (SED: 66).

Imagery

Baudrillard might be said here to be hypersensitive to the shift involved, to what is eliminated – the public sphere of direct political argument and debate (SED: 67). What is eliminated in a virtual war is the direct encounter with the other: henceforth the lethal encounter is a screen image. From an analysis of the generalisation of these technical processes (statistical, virtual, and so on) Baudrillard attempts to show that unexpectedly significant cultural and social transitions are occurring. The terminology adopted to show this does not suggest that there is a new layer of representation between the processes of interaction and the event itself. There is no harmonious or homogeneous transition occurring between these levels. The emergence of the new media interposes a new order of social space-time with new characteristics, for which conventional social science is unable to theorise from its own conceptual resources.

In his 1978 essay *In the Shadow of the Silent Majorities* Baudrillard uses a blitz of such terms: the masses are full of currents and flows, they are the earth for electrical impulses, they absorb radiation, they form an 'opaque nebula whose growing density absorbs all the surrounding energy and light rays, to collapse finally under its own weight. A black hole which engulfs the social' (ISSM: 3–4). After passages such as that Baudrillard comments: the term mass 'is a lumpenanalytical concept' and any attempt to define it is a 'mistake – it is to provide meaning for that which has none' (ISSM: 5). The logic of this position stems from the fact that the masses are a 'statistical refuse. The mass is without attribute, predicate, quality, reference. This is ... its radical lack of definition' (ISSM: 5). As a concept it is not part of traditional sociology: in fact, he argues, 'this is, therefore, exactly the reverse of a "sociological" understanding' (ISSM: 4). On the other hand it is clear that Baudrillard reaches a conclusion that is dramatically sociological, or more precisely one that has significant sociological implications: ' ... it is impossible for the mass to be alienated, since neither the one nor the other exist there any longer ... The mass is what remains when the social has been completely removed' (ISSM: 6). Baudrillard's position is, then, a highly calculated attempt to work out a new kind of theorising for a new type of phenomenon: what happens to a society in which the forces at work produce a regime in which, as Margaret Thatcher (who came to power in 1979) was to say: 'There is no such thing as society.'

Baudrillard talks of the right image, the right metaphor for this transformation: the image of the mass as mirror of the social is 'not right, since it evokes the idea of ... resistance'. The better image is that of 'a gigantic black hole which inexorably inflects, bends and distorts all energy and light radiation ... an implosive sphere, in which the curvature of spaces accelerates, in which all dimensions curve back on themselves' (ISSM: 9). Evidently Baudrillard adopts a new poetics, raiding the concepts becoming available in physics and mathematics. Whether or not the new poetics is effective, it can certainly be maintained that its adoption simply followed the development of new mathematical techniques of mass media inquiry, and of communication and information technologies. Baudrillard concludes ' ... an admirable conjunction, between those who have nothing to say, and the masses, who do not speak' (ISSM: 6). The mass, produced as a statistical probability, is neither a subject nor an object (ISSM: 30ff.).

It makes little sense to argue that Baudrillard introduced concepts from physics in an inappropriate way, or that his use of them is sloppy (as argued by Sokal and Bricmont): they are explicitly presented as 'lumpenanalytical'. They are probably not used with high degrees of exactness or even consistency. The central issue for Baudrillard is whether they are used with sufficient force to evoke the shift that he wants to think about, whether this is within a realm of scientific discourse or not. Baudrillard takes the move towards the dissolution of the traditional separation of object and subject of research in 'the ultimate analysis ... the horizon of microphysics ... where the subject of observation is himself annulled' (ISSM: 31). It must be emphasised throughout that all these analyses are framed within an account of the movement of Western culture: in the essay of 1978 on the silent majorities, the analysis revolved around the hyper-conformity of the masses and attempts to measure their opinions. By 1990 Baudrillard was writing that that stage had been 'still nihilistic', but that this had changed: 'where the masses once sported with their voluntary servitude, they now sport with their involuntary incertitude ... The masses had been deliberately demoralized and de-ideologized in order that they might become the live prey of probability theory, but now it is they who destabilize all images and play games with political truth ... the masses are an incarnation, on the margins, of the principle of uncertainty in the sociological sphere' (TE: 41).

Uncertainty

Again Baudrillard seems to like to identify beginnings: ' ... the natural sciences were the first to describe a panic situation of this kind: ... the disappearance of the respective positions of subject and object at the experimental interface that has given rise to a definitive state of uncertainty' (TE: 42). He instances all those processes where the handling of large quantities of data and information are closely interwoven with the management of systems, whether economic, social or political, which with the introduction of statistical and information manipulation in the production of their 'objects' do exactly the same thing. The system becomes a hostage to its own tautologies. Baudrillard's images are not altogether consistent, for this is described as a system of branchings into infinity, but also as an infinite circularity with the symbol for infinity in the form of a Moebius band. Both of these are images for the new space-time produced by the new technologies.

The key image is not that of the simple loss of the traditionally secure identity of subject and object. It is rather the sudden loss of the capacity to identify at the same time the speed and position of an object. Baudrillard takes up the question of uncertainty as introduced by Heisenberg. If we take a recent popular presentation of what is at stake here, we read: 'A Universe running according to Newtonian physics is deterministic, in the sense that if we knew the positions and velocities of all the particles in a system at a given time, we could predict their behavior at all subsequent times ... ' (the familiar world of social science as well). But 'in a world according to quantum theory, every entity has a dual nature ... real entities ... behave sometimes as if they were waves and sometimes as if they were particles ... Heisenberg's uncertainty principle states that ... the better we know the position x, the less well we know the momentum p' (Coles 1998: 301–3).

In fact the idea of the speed and position of an object seems to have a parallel in social theory in a long-standing debate about diachronic and synchronic analyses. Even at the beginning of sociology Comte made the separation between what he called social dynamics and social statics the cornerstone of his methodology. Marx also, as Althusser demonstrated, introduced a strict separation between genealogy and system analysis. In Saussure, linguistic functioning is synchronic, and the analysis of diachronic laws is quite distinct. However, in all these cases the theoretical conceptions are developed within a strictly deterministic universe. Comte in particular rejected all attempts to introduce techniques of probability into sociology, even at the margin. Because of the insistence on the necessity for a principle of determinism and the reality principle, attempts to analyse historical development, as Popper showed in the case of Comte, and Althusser showed in the case of Marxism, almost always fall into the simple tracing of empirical sequences so that the diachrony and synchrony are mapped together.

Baudrillard's theorising tries to move into a more rigorous alignment with the logic of Heisenberg's uncertainty principle. This is evidently not an application of the principle in the sense of reducing social events to physics, but of the principle of the uncertainty consequent on the withdrawal of the reality principle (Euclidean space-time, mechanical or expressive cause–effect relations) from the analysis of dynamics and statics. If we stand back from these issues, Baudrillard attempts to show that, in its own way, the uncertainty principle is itself reproduced from within contemporary culture: we would expect to find leading trends within theory moving towards methods of calculation and analysis which begin to mirror the dissolution of the traditional subject–object separation. If we define the determined world as modern, the shift into the principle of uncertainty is emblematic of postmodernity.

Postmodern science?

But this is not in fact what Baudrillard does, at least in any simple sense. His analysis of nihilism suggests that the nineteenth century was dominated by the destruction of appearances (this is modernity), while the twentieth century is dominated by the destruction of meaning (postmodernity). This second stage is beyond nihilism, which belongs to a determined world heading for catastrophe. In the twentieth century, he argues, it is uncertainty, the aleatoric, which becomes the rule (SS: 159). By 1989 Baudrillard noted that postmodernism destroys but also recreates; it involves 'a restoration in distortion' since it 'functions via this unpredictability, and by means of [the] lack of events'. It is therefore the 'most degenerated, most artificial and most eclectic phase – a picking out and adopting of all the significant little bits and pieces, all the idols, and purest signs that preceded this fetishism' (LBEW: 40–1). Baudrillard stigmatises postmodernism as decadence; and having taken this position, he does not follow Lyotard in describing the new regime in science as a development into postmodernism, even though the natural sciences are described as 'the first' to define the 'uncertainty which lies at the core of the present operational euphoria' (TE: 42). The term 'postmodernism' is reserved consistently for the culture of repentance, of recycling, but also for the culture of consensus where 'in the East and the West, the Idea is finished. The organic consensus marks the dawn of post-modern societies, non-conflictual and at one with themselves' (IE: 41).

Against this consensual form Baudrillard finds in the advanced sciences instances of extreme thought, and these occur not in post-modernity but in 'extreme' radical modernity (IE: 117). Thus if there is the restoration of older forms within extreme modernity 'their resurrection is itself hyper-real. The resuscitated values are themselves fluid, unstable ... the rehabilitation of ... the old structures, old elites will therefore never have the same meaning. If one day the aristocracy or royalty recover their old position, they will, nonetheless, be "post-modern"' (IE: 117). It is as if the more fundamental shift into indeterminacy, which is registered through a series of structural effects and reversals, is accompanied by a whole array of secondary cultural modifications which are mocked unrelentingly by Baudrillard as 'postmodern': such as 'the exalting of residues, rehabilitation by bricolage, eclectic sentimentality ... high dilution and low intensities' (IE: 35). These postmodern forms proliferate throughout Western culture and even its economic structures (IE: 36).

In this sense, then, Baudrillard has certainly made a significant gesture towards rejecting 'postmodernism'; indeed, towards positioning himself in alliance with the vigorous and extreme developments in the natural and life sciences against postmodernism. His description of the instabilities of postmodern culture always refer to something 'floating' and virtual, incoherent and shifting, eclectic; and to a culture described as 'rediscovering love, selflessness, togetherness, international compassion, and the individual tremolo' – these are not the 'hard ideologies nor radical philosophies' of earlier periods (LBEW: 43). This is the culture of soft indeterminacy, eclectic fusion and comfortable confusion. The postmodern as poly- and multi-culturalism, of 'total eclectism' (Ibid.). There is here a loss of boundaries through interpenetration, intermixing, mingling, through indifference and loss of strongly defined value spheres. In this situation there is 'an air-conditioned intelligence that tries to avoid passing the threshold of a breach' (LBEW: 42). It seems that Baudrillard could not make his rejection of this postmodern condition of 'gentle ideologies' and weak indeterminacy any clearer. His option is to have moved into a condition of radical uncertainty, parallel to that universe conceived in the hard and radical ideologies of the sciences.

But there is also another reading of the postmodern condition, which Baudrillard is keen to avoid and to disassociate himself from. This is the entry into the pure realm of chaos and the aleatoric itself. Now here there is no attack on the mathematics of chaos and probabilities in terms of their internal eclecticism. Sokal and Bricmont admit that they are at a total loss to understand this, noting that terminology taken from science is 'inserted in sentences that are, as far as we can make out, devoid of meaning' (Sokal & Bricmont 1998: 142). In the long passage they cite, Sokal and Bricmont miss out two key paragraphs of the argument (IE: 112–13), where Baudrillard makes the distinction between the idea of destiny and that of chance. In theories of chaos which are theories of the aleatoric, there can be eccentric and catastrophic effects (cf. Deleuze). Baudrillard is not situated here: for him these are effects which arise in cultures which lose an overarching sense of fate, destiny and necessity. Chance then is really only a secondary figuration, it is 'a parody of any metaphysics of destiny'. Thus the strange attractor is only strange as metaphor, and even as a 'hidden order' of processes of chaotic randomness strange attractors are outside of the fatal order itself. Indeed, banal chaos can only proliferate 'when destiny is absent'. Baudrillard's formula is that 'chaos is merely the metastatic figure of Chance' (IE: 113).

Thus it is clear that Baudrillard also stands outside the scientific ideologies of randomness and chaotic processes. His reasoning can be reconstructed by referring back to the distinction between the Newtonian and Heisenbergian universes and the meaning of mortality and immortality. When the ordered universe

> begins to break up ... the cosmic order, like the human order, emancipated from God and all finality, becomes shifting and unstable ... The happy consciousness of eternity and immortality is ended. The problem of the end becomes crucial and insoluble.

There will no longer be an end. We enter upon a kind of radical interdeterminacy. (IE: 91, Baudrillard's emphasis).

Baudrillard then is quite specific: 'all the extreme phenomena ... the destiny of simulation ... read as a form of catastrophe of reality' is only a perverse logic. In these processes there are only exponential effects, eccentricity, 'indefinite fractal scissiparity' which cannot reach an end point. 'They are condemned, precisely to the epidemic' (IE: 114). In this passage, there is a blitz of terminology which revolves around one idea, the repetition of a process into infinity: intense metabolism, metastasis, indefinite scissiparity, proliferation, and so on. These can all be fascinating merely as 'extreme phenomena, exorbitant effects, vertiginous forms of disorder'. Fascination in the face of catastrophe is quite different, however, from that involvement in destiny which Baudrillard describes as the 'ecstatic figure of necessity' (IE: 113). What is it that Sokal and Bricmont suggest is 'devoid of meaning'? It is the distinction between the order of destiny and that of chaos. Of course if it is meaningless then so too are all those cultures and world religions which make this distinction. It is not Sokal and Bricmont's case that this distinction is false: they say that it is 'devoid of meaning'.

Sokal and Bricmont notice that this distinction is discussed elsewhere by Baudrillard and they cite another long extract. It is a passage taken from *Fatal Strategies*, in which Baudrillard argues that science goes beyond the revolution of the uncertainty principle, which he calls the first revolution, to develop a sense of 'a possible reversibility of physical laws' (Sokal & Bricmont 1998: 139). The problems posed here are that of the nature of reversibility itself and how laws themselves might be reversible. It is true that it is extremely difficult to understand what Baudrillard might mean by the latter. It is not difficult to grasp the meaning of reversibility itself: Baudrillard's key example is anthropological, the exchange of gifts as analysed by Mauss. The order of the gift is not chaotic: it is fatal and reversible (gift and counter-gift, obligation and release from obligation). This is symbolic exchange in ritualised culture. Where this culture no longer functions, secular and profane randomness takes the place of destiny, and because there is no structure of reversibility there is proliferation and accumulation. Baudrillard asks: 'what if even physical laws ... are slipping so gently into the reversible? In any case it is from this reversibility ... and not from chance ... that we must expect a surprise' (FS: 164). This certainly indicates where Baudrillard is looking: the analysis of radical uncertainty is only the examination of certain conditions of possibility.

CHAPTER 6

Bathos of Technology

> We ... labour under the illusion that the aim of technology
> is to be an extension of man and his power. (CMII: 71)

According to Jean Baudrillard we have entered a new situation, one
he calls the fourth order of simulacra. In a 'precession' of simulacra
which mocks the genealogies developed by Nietzsche, Benjamin, and
Foucault, he proposes the *trompe l'oeil* and automaton as the false–
true of a first simulacral order (the initiation here brings into existence
the 'real' itself as a simulacrum); the second is the order of mass
reproduction; the third comprises mass media (hyperreal) representation
and simulation techniques; while today we have entered a fourth fractal,
or viral order. 'Let me introduce a new particle into the microphysics
of simulacra', he wrote in 1992; 'after the natural, commodity, and
structural stages comes the fractal stage ... At the fourth, the fractal
stage of value there is no point of reference at all, and value radiates
in all directions, occupying all interstices ... properly speaking there
is now no law of value' (in Stearns & Chaloupka 1992: 5–6) – no false
(because no determinate) standard of truth, good, health, and so on,
remains intact. Few commentators have registered their agreement
with Baudrillard here. Genosko concludes that the way Baudrillard
theorises this fourth order does not 'tell us anything about the nature
of the culture of the fourth order. [It] ... is a licence to generalize on a
pathological model' (Genosko 1994: 54–5). There is even less discussion
of the political implications of this thesis and Baudrillard's effort to
outline a radical response (see PC: 94–105).

Fourth order

But what exactly is involved in the thesis that there has been a seismic
shift away from the code, hyperreality, and so on, to the virtual, the fractal,
viral, to a proliferation and dispersal of value where 'good is no longer
the opposite of evil' where 'each fragment of value shines for a moment
in the heavens of simulation, then disappears into the void along a
crooked path that only rarely happens to intersect with other such paths'
(TE: 6)? Is this not simply an escalation in a frustrated, even exasperated,
rhetoric of political despair, expressed through a changing but always
inappropriate language of postmodern pseudo-science and technophobia?

A new mode of exposition corresponding to the new order is adopted by Baudrillard: of announcing at the same time quite opposed competing theses on our current predicament, insisting that it has become simply an impossible task to decide which one of them is right. The world is speeding up, the world is slowing down; the economy is dominant, culture is dominant; the media manipulates the masses, the masses manipulate the media. The nature of the social, whether it exists or not, becomes undecidable. The same is true of technology, for 'technology has taken into itself all the illusion it has caused us to lose, and ... what we have in return ... is the emergence of an objective irony of this world ... the radical illusion of technology' (PC: 72). This is now as plausible a proposition as its contrary. Third-order theory suggested that the irony of the new situation can be found in the fact that the initiative is with technology, as it fashions us via its own functions, its own obscure ends, and thus subverts and diverts the sovereignty of the human. Baudrillard's analysis of the fourth dimension suggests that the principle of uncertainty makes this irony itself dependent on purely aleatoric contiguities. This leads, he argues, to an unprecedented configuration, to a culture and politics in radical uncertainty, politics enters a situation where it is not possible to envisage any exchange against an ideal end, only against its virtual double. But then the totality, the world, is no longer one. This is the thesis of the end of the law of value: exchanges are impossible since there is only 'radical non-equivalence' or clone-like replication. Critical and revolutionary theory is redundant in the face of eccentric singularities. The world in which real could be exchanged with real, or thought with political programme, becomes more than problematic in an aleatoric universe.

It has often been said that Baudrillard, like McLuhan before him, is simply caught in the trap of a technological determinism. If he is, of course, it will now be in a completely new way, for even as a thesis this too becomes as plausible as its opposite, or its alternatives. In the past, in periods of an ascendant technology the world appeared an unproblematic reality: but on 'the downward curve – or because the movement is simply continuing as a result of its own inertia – everything is caught in a different refraction space, as in a gravity alternator' (PC: 66). Politically the second order, the age of revolution, of class struggle, of history, rested on the energies invested in and derived from hierarchical but secure class bases of social action and representation. In third-order simulacra, class energies implode into the mass, into an inert silence which nevertheless acts as a dense gravity for the political. For Baudrillard the political left (and he was on the ultra-left) failed because 'it was not capable of coming to terms with the indifference and inertia of the social body. For its part the Right identifies spontaneously with this inert phantom' (FCM: 63). In fourth-order Western politics, this left–right split breaks down ('beyond left and right', says Giddens) as politics enters definitively into a transpolitical epoch: into the movement of fragments, strange and extreme combinations of dissolving forms. Take Europe: it is for Baudrillard the 'very archetype of the contemporary event: a vacuum-packed phantasmagoria ... Europe as virtual reality, to be slipped into like a datasuit' (FCM: 51).

Baudrillard's brilliant charting of the shifts from mass production (second-order simulacra also including the produced notion of the 'real' and 'reality' principles) to hyperreality and simulation (third-order dissolutions of the subject–object distinction, but also supporting the continuity of the real), seems at first sight to be incoherent in the fourth (the fractal and the viral, where the object thinks the human). Baudrillard still appears to be thinking this through and working on the idea, rather as 'physicists who invent – I do say invent and not discover – a new particle each month' (in Stearns & Chaloupka 1992: 15). The problem is that for the reader the thesis of the fourth order is, as a conception and definition, still *in statu nascendi*. Just as Baudrillard's theory of hyperreality (and the end of the social) took over a decade to be seen as having caught the shift that has occurred in our societies, something of the same disbelief hangs over this thesis. Baudrillard's ideas are nothing if not dramatic: when images could be reproduced mechanically (Benjamin 1970: 219ff.), 'reproduction precedes production', the extensions of man were still external, or *exotechnical*; but with 'the technological sophistication of our own era', particularly the technology of cloning, prostheses have become internal, and *esotechnical*. 'Ours is the age of soft technologies, the age of genetic and mental software' where the body is 'nothing more than computer fodder' (PC: 118–19). As the nature of the totality changes, this too becomes useless and is eliminated: 'if all information is contained in each of its parts, the whole loses significance' (PC: 116). It is this loss which introduces the possibility of simulation of a new kind. Whereas the technology of traditional prostheses was essentially mechanical, and this mechanical addition could be the subject of simulation (and therefore still an 'extension of man'), so it may be that some time in the mid to late 1980s another shift took place in which through acceleration, or its opposite, the world finished with its capacity to deal with definitive and unequivocal values: there is no longer 'any law of value as such, dialectical or structural' (in Stearns & Chaloupka 1992: 16). The revolution in genetics typically catches this relation: the body becomes an extension of the molecule. The body reproduced in perfected forms is only a moment in a possible 'infinite series of prostheses' (TE: 117).

These new ideas of Baudrillard have not attracted much in the way of interpretative commentary, and in what criticism there is, the third and fourth orders of simulation tend to get conflated. It is clear that for Baudrillard the theory of the third order does not adequately align with or correspond to the increasingly violent transformations in technology and science, and the specific transformations in politics. It is important to remember that Baudrillard was quick to see the implications of cloning in the 1970s. An essay of 1979 (see SS: 95–103, reproduced with a new conclusion in TE: 113–23) outlined a position on cloning which suggested that here the sexual function of the father and mother are replaced by the matrix of the code, 'an operational mode from which all chance sexual elements have been expunged', as well as the otherness of the twin in the 'reiteration of the same' (TE: 115–16). Baudrillard in 1979 had to resort to an industrial image to express this complexity: 'an individual product on the conveyor belt is in no sense a reflection of the next (albeit identical) product in line', so 'far from widening an aleatory freedom for the subject' there is 'just a matrix' (TE: 115). Baudrillard's new conclusion to this essay adopts the classic terms he has now developed for the fourth order: 'Without the Other as mirror, as reflecting surface, consciousness of self is threatened with irradiation in the void ... Division has been replaced with mere propagation. And whereas the other may always conceal a second other, the Same never conceals anything but itself. This is our clone-ideal today: a subject purged of the other, deprived of its divided character and doomed to self-metastasis, to pure repetition. No longer the hell of other people, but the hell of the same' (TE: 122). At issue is the way in which many of the elements already identified in the third order are carried over into a new and unprecedented situation. One might say that Baudrillard is trying to read off the more deeply lying transformation in culture and politics through the paradoxes introduced in science and technology, insisting that processes are proceeding in a strict parallelism in all domains.

Baudrillard's conception of the fourth order of simulacra, as noted, suggests that one of its key features is the increasing impossibility of deciding between theories and hypotheses. At the beginning of his book *The Illusion of the End* for example, his essay 'Pataphysics of the Year 2000' presents three plausible reasons to account for the end of history. The first is the thesis that events have speeded up to such an extent they have reached an escape velocity, so that 'all atoms of meaning get lost in space' (IE: 2). The second thesis is that, on the contrary, the density of a mass or the saturation of highways and superhighways of communication has slowed history down to the point of stasis. The third thesis concerns the increasing perfection of technology itself. His surprisingly homely example is that of the technology of musical reproduction, hi-fi equipment. 'At the consoles of our stereos, armed with our tuners, amplifiers and speakers, we mix, adjust settings, multiply tracks in pursuit of a flawless sound. Is this still music?' For Baudrillard, still astonished by these developments, hi-fi technology brings about the 'ecstasy of music', suggesting that beyond a certain point music 'disappears into the perfection of its materiality ... its own special effect' (IE: 5). This image of the technical perfection of musical reproduction has haunted Baudrillard for some time and results in a surprising bathos: for here he discovers a negative holocaust, 'objects from which wear-and-tear, death or ageing have been eradicated' (IE: 101).

It would be too facile to think that this is an affected technophobia. Baudrillard's relation to the object is not experienced as a fetishism of commodities. It is rather an anthropological experience of the object as fetish. The fetish as strange attractor, as powerfully auratic. The irony of technology is a strategy of the object on the condition of a radicalisation of the power of the fetish. But this very condition permits the reappearance of the figure of anticlimax, an effect of pure contiguity, a figure to be encountered more and more frequently perhaps in the fourth order of simulacra: 'The compact disc. It doesn't wear out, even if you use it. Terrifying ... It's as though you'd never used it. It's as though you didn't exist' (IE: 101).

Bathos

What are the transpolitical forms of the fourth order? Most commentators are fascinated by Baudrillard's analysis of the Gulf War (which 'sought to reopen the space of war, the space of a violence that could establish a new world order' and which did not happen, and so on (IE: 117)), or more rarely with his analysis of Bosnia (which concerns the demarcation of the Western zone by the Serbs, a complicity hypocritically denied by Europe (see PC: 132–8, and the essays in Cushman & Mestrovic 1996: 79–89)). It seems as if Baudrillard here is still charged up with a critical power to denounce the complex combination of human rights ideology, indulgent and hypocritical pity for victims, an impotent politics, but above all an attempt to impose on the world 'in the guise of universals ... not its disjointed values, but its lack of values' (in Cushman & Mestrovic 1996: 86). But we have entered the era of both indifference and extreme phenomena, and the radical uncertainty arising from doubly chaotic processes (exponential stability and instability: two states which are incompatible but strangely indifferent to the fact that they are 'simultaneously valid' (IE: 112)).

From issues of war we can pass directly to political meteorology. As Baudrillard points out, weather forecasting is dominated by chaos theory, with the 'disproportion between the beating of the butterfly's wings and the hurricane this unleashes on the other side of the world' (IE: 110). But Baudrillard is one of the few theorists who looks to examine things by reversing the expected mode of analysis. For example, why, he asks of readers of political zodiacs, 'don't we accord more importance to the star signs of death? It's barely imaginable that the star sign you are going to die under doesn't exert an anticipatory power equal to the one you were born under ... ' (PC: 72). So it is completely to be expected that in discussing the political implications of chaos theory he should ask, 'has any concern been shown in chaos theory ... [for] the inverse exponentiality of effects in relation to causes – the potential hurricanes which end in the beating of a butterfly's wings?' (IE: 114). In posing the question, he has formulated precisely, at least, a new conceptualisation of bathos: inverse exponentiality. In his reflections on meteorology, he suggests that the weather report, with satellite information support conjuring up a simulated scenario of the weather, now redefines all that can be seen from the window, in a classic shift towards a new type of political analysis (ET: 97ff.). There is a curious outcome typified perhaps by an example from sport: we see on screen a clear case of one football player kicking another, while the official commentary, even as we watch it happening, says it is not happening. We see on the screen the hyper-chao-tech prediction that the weather outside is wet, we look out of the window and see it is dry. Note that what we see as 'real' is now in a field of perception determined by the prediction.

Each political formation arises on the basis of a criminal event (a revolution, a regicide). For Baudrillard the imperfect crime of extreme modernity (PC: 40) is the catastrophe of the virtualisation of the world. Against Derrida and Virilio, he argues that this apocalypse has already happened, so that an apocalypse in the real is now an impossibility. But in the virtual almost anything is possible including the 'rehabilitation of the old frontiers, the old structures, the old elites ... [and] if one day, the aristocracy or royalty recover their old position, they will, nonetheless, be "post-modern"' (IE: 117). Thus the (im)perfect crime which makes the fourth order possible, yet its imperfections haunt it throughout: a final solution for reality, and the dissipation of its energy. The human may exist through these very traces of imperfection.

Yet this may be too optimistic. The fourth order may be a slightly different beast. Instead of uncertainty theory, chaos, and fractal dimensions providing us with a radical uncertainty leading to indifference, these new shifts in physics and mathematics seem to be even more productive than their forerunners, at least in certain domains. In other words, instead of making the world more difficult to control and to order, these techniques bring a more subtle invention of technical mastery. Far from being feared and rejected by business and government, these techniques are embraced as providing new powers of prediction (see Anderla et al. 1997). Certainly Baudrillard is right to point to the specific kind of vision invented here, and the fundamental shift involved in the hegemony of uncertainty over certainty, fractal over fraction, the fact is that this heightens mathematical control, 'an uncertainty principle which can be mastered by equations' (PC: 55). Simple opposition to these developments reproduces the attempts of socio-mathematicians such as Auguste Comte to prevent the development of statistics and probability theory in the early nineteenth century.

Hitherto the orders of simulacra have been contrasted with the primordial forms of the symbolic order, and this has always given

Baudrillard's work a romantic and nostalgic character. But in his recent works the concept of the symbolic has been developed towards Nietzsche's notion of the vital illusion of the world, while some of the forms he previously lodged in the symbolic have been rediscovered in the extreme phenomena of the cosmic order. If this is true, his more fundamental project is to find a space of play in which radical theory disturbs the ways in which the new sciences of uncertainty produce specific if paradoxical forms of mastery. The one Baudrillard prefers is the rediscovery of reversibility at the heart of these sciences: if the world is essentially the product of a certain type of, say, mathematical and technological method that breaks down the conventional opposition between subject and object, it now becomes entirely possible to suggest that it is the object which discovers the subject.

What kind of world-view is this? On the one hand it is a step back from mono-centrism towards a re-enchanted world – through neo-fetishism and perhaps neo-polytheism (see here Baudrillard's (re)adoption of the anagrammatic dispersal of the names of the Gods (PC: 100, and SED: 195–222)). On the other, it is a disenchantment with the attempt to create a perfect technological mastery and simulation of the world. This latter possibility is addressed with great seriousness: the virtualisation of the world is the apocalypse. But a now familiar bathos constantly reappears, for if mankind takes the opportunity to disappear behind technology, the deletion of the world into its perfect simulacra would be complete: 'the video plugged into the TV takes over the job of watching the film ... These machines are all marvellous ... They relieve him of his own production: what a relief to see twenty pages that had been stored in memory wiped out at a stroke ... What the computer had given ... – perhaps too easily – it takes away with the same ease' (PC: 40–1). It turns out then that it is not clear if the human has invested the world with 'uncertainty' and imperfection, or the reverse, which is the fundamental uncertainty. These consequences undo the totality and all totalisation, made impossible by the simultaneous explosion and implosion of vectors. Baudrillard is consistent here in arguing that 'there is irony in all extreme processes' and that what is new is that the irony in the present situation is one 'which plays not on negation but on empty positivity, on exponential platitude, to the point where the process turns around of its own accord and rediscovers the splendour of the void' (PC: 70). Is this the new anti-environment of inverse exponentiality? What counts as a 'real' political event 'occurs in a vacuum, stripped of its context and only visible from afar, televisually', leading to the pure political event itself: 'no one will have directly experienced the actual course of such happenings, but everyone will have received an image of them' (TE: 80). And everyone, perhaps, will also be deprived of an image of them.

Strange political effects then might be expected in this scenario. On the one hand, indifference, particularly that arising from the disappearance of the social. A savage conformism (around a fetishised system of differences) in the reproduction of mass conformity, cynically exploited by political states (Baudrillard identifies the means: 'intimidation, dissuasion, simulation, provocation or spectacular solicitation' (TE: 79)). But, on the other, we witness the appearance of extreme effects engendered here as 'phobic' relations with idealised others, either as negative panics (hatred of extremes) or positive enthusiasms (from humanitarian and socialist attempts to identify and save victims to extreme idolisations like the Diana cult, and football fanaticism), and since these are founded on an idealisation the 'relationship is an exponential one' (PC: 132). Baudrillard's attempt to produce a radical response to this fourth order continues the idea of poetic resolution (Saussure) carried over from his 1970s writing, but recontextualised within the Nietzschean notion of the radical illusion of the world. This leads to Baudrillard's strategy: theory must 'advance behind a mask and constitute itself as a decoy ... [i]t is the world itself which must reveal itself not as truth but as illusion' (PC: 99). Although there is no account in Baudrillard's writings of a radical politics, there seems little doubt that its form would be the same as his radical theory. We are a long way from the revolutionary project, the game has gone beyond transgression to extremes. And 'all of the advanced technological process points up the fact that behind his ... virtual images, man takes advantage of these things to disappear. So it is with the answer-phone: "We aren't in. Leave a message ... "' (PC: 40).

CHAPTER 7

Sex and Gender

> This invention of difference coincides with
> the invention of a new image of woman,
> and thus a change of sexual paradigm. (PC: 116)

Baudrillard has earned a reputation for being one of the very few contemporary French intellectuals of left-wing background to oppose feminism: some pour scorn on him as a curious, backward and immoral figure; others have welcomed a degree of honesty and openness, albeit reactionary in inspiration. This chapter does not intend to discuss whether Catholic French society is more or less patriarchal than that of, say, Britain or the USA, or whether the feminist movements have been more or less successful in the Protestant cultures. It is more narrowly concerned, first, with examining some of the curious elements in Baudrillard's position and looking at some of the ways in which this position has been interpreted in the English speaking cultures, and secondly with examining Baudrillard's position in the context of some French responses to feminism and the crisis of masculinity.

Feminism

From 1968 to 1976 Baudrillard's dominant interest was in the sociology of the affluent society and consumerism, and in developing a position that a new phase of capitalism had commenced with new forms of object consumption and repressive desublimation. One important aspect of this discussion was an analysis of the so-called sexual revolution and the emancipation of women (CS: 136). Although his position at the time was one of revolutionary opposition to the consumer society on the basis of class and culture, Baudrillard's attitude to the prevailing form of the liberation of women was always hostile. His view was that just at the moment of 'emancipation', the coincidence with consumerism began to exercise a new enslavement, as women became linked with the pleasure principle of the new society. Women became trapped within the new beauty system, the terrain of a vast new industry of mass-media image manipulation and selling. And at the sexual level, all the previous restraints of the symbolic cultures were swept away in promiscuity and pornography. The impact of the feminist movement was also to induce a kind of feminisation of the whole of Western culture.

His interpretation of these issues changed dramatically with the appearance of his book *Seduction*, first published in France in 1979. A number of fundamental modifications of his conceptions had occurred. Gone was the idea that modern cultures could be regarded as dominated by a historical dialectic, or could be criticised from the position of symbolic cultures, though it is clear that these notions survive as important reference points of his thought. His new position was to attempt to find in modern cultures sites where the headlong rush into 'hyperreality' could be confronted. His tactic was to attempt a new kind of analysis which gave predominance to the 'object' over the subject and to find in the object a new basis for opposition to the 'ecstatic' forms which had replaced those associated with alienation. This shift, he argued, had instantly reduced all progressive politics to irrelevance, since they belong to an era of historical and dialectical struggles based on the assumption of the dominance of the constitutive subject. It is the object which now appears centre stage, and to understand this it is necessary to move from the principle that the world is produced by the subject, to one which holds that the world is seduced by the object. The object is no longer seen as passive and inert, but is now active and ironically resists and subverts the subject. Nature will no longer willingly oblige the scientist by conforming to theories or technologies. Just at the moment of greatest control and mastery, the object takes its revenge. Thus we pass from the heroic world of progressive revolution to the imploding world of catastrophe, without hope of transcendence.

But if transcendence is now impossible it means we are in a one-dimensional world with a vengeance. Whereas Marcuse's famous one-dimensional world (at least in the book with that title of 1964) sees little in the way of possible intervention, Baudrillard has sought to find some principle of action. From about 1979 the problem is posed as one of understanding the nature of seduction, and it is here that the confrontation with feminism really begins. Baudrillard wants to identify the principle of seduction as feminine, as having been mastered by women since the beginning of history. Women have used seduction to checkmate 'masculine profundity' and have triumphed: against the feminine, men have set up the fortresses of masculine institutions, a sure index of their real fragility. Seduction is not mysterious, it is enigmatic. Via the challenge its stake escalates to the limit. But it functions on the level of appearances, the 'superficial abyss'. Baudrillard is interested in the superficial not because he wishes to preserve the profundity of the male, but because his theory suggests that the cultural order in the West has reached, decisively, a stage which has eliminated depth and profundity (the world of Marx) in favour of one-dimensional superficial hyperreality. Baudrillard wants to pass over to the order of seduction and counter-seduction so as to found a completely new kind of poetic-fatal theory which may strike at the hyperreal. Ironically he wants to make this move just as women abandon objectality in favour of equality and identity.

The problem is that Baudrillard is, or so he thinks, one step ahead of the critical progressives and feminists, who are still struggling to put some new substance into the emancipatory project. For him, the soft ideologies of ecologism, anti-racism, peace, love, socialism, humanism and the 'individual tremolo' are a regrouping of the dominant forms of *ressentiment* alongside the emergence of the 'European yuppies' and cultural 'postmodernism'. The *mélange* of elements here, he argues, only indicates the loss of strong values, the devaluation of meaning and accelerating entropy: the debauchery of signs. One feminist, Meaghan Morris, finds in Baudrillard at least a grim honesty. She takes up one of his minor theoretical illustrations of fatal seduction, which is 'set in some vague courtly contest with the ambience of a mid eighteenth century epistolary novel in which a man is trying to seduce a woman. She asks 'which part of me do you find most seductive?' He replies 'your eyes'. Next day, he received an envelope. Inside, instead of the letter, he receives a bloody eye. Morris notes that Baudrillard has hoped to show that the 'woman has purloined the place of the seducer ... the woman's literalness is fatal to the man's banal figuration ... Nonetheless, in making the pun, she loses an eye, but he loses face. Baudrillard in fact enunciatively reoccupies the place of control of meaning by deliteralising the woman's gesture, and returning it to figuration' (Morris 1988: 188f.). Every attempt to present the exchanges in the process of seduction only artificially arrives at equivalent values. But then this an aristocratic and deadly game.

Baudrillard's complex feelings are apparent in an account of a moment of confrontation at a seminar. At this particular seminar, there is both a feminist and a disabled student. He makes it clear that his antagonism to the disabled male student is intense (CM: 104–5). Baudrillard describes how the woman 'sat down next to the handicapped man and throughout her (aggressive) argument leaned tenderly toward him, slipping a lit cigarette in and out of his mouth to enable him to smoke ... Beautiful, provocative girl doling out her little revenge through a poor, impotent polio case. And him glowing painfully with the pleasure of this unexpected rape ... she was soliciting me as she practically masturbated him before my eyes, she was saying to me ... "I am raping you through him and there's nothing you can do about it".' Baudrillard admits this was 'a stroke of genius'. Douglas Kellner, outraged by this account, wrote: 'Baudrillard lets it all hang out – shamelessly, unrepentently good Nietzschean aristocrat to the core. No compassion for the suffering or willingness to engage in dialogue with feminism' (Kellner 1989: 182–4). Whether Baudrillard thinks he won the argument on seduction at this seminar we do not know. What he does tell us is that the feminist brilliantly inverted the situation as she placed Baudrillard in the position he least wanted. However, in so presenting the scene as a defeat for himself, Baudrillard, of course, also wishes to subvert the apparent victory of the feminist: she practised the art which he preached, thus providing the proof he needed for the deadly game of seduction and the triumph of the object. 'I love that woman who shamelessly exploited a disabled man to promote her shitty feminism, as I love that other woman who ... offered her eye to her lover as a response to a compliment' (CM: 82).

Baudrillard evidently seeks to provoke the humanist and feminist consensus. Meaghan Morris points to the problem of metaphor and its apparently asymmetrical uses between the genders. Baudrillard is perhaps even more extreme than might be credited. In one section of his journal he reports a case from 1981 of 'sentimental cannibalism'. Issei Sagawa invited a young Dutch girl to a meal and then to read poetry. As she reads he shoots her, and then eats her. After a two-day 'repast', 'professing undying love, Issei Sagawa lay down on a bench and fell asleep'. Baudrillard remarks:

> the silence of metaphor accompanies the cruel act, thus the Japanese cannibal passed directly from the metaphor of love to the devouring of that marvelous young Dutch girl. Or that woman who made a gift of her eye to the man who told her how much he appreciated her look. The effacement of metaphor is characteristic of the object and its cruelty. The words show only a material, literal tenor. They are not any more signs of a language. It is the silence of pure objectality. (CM: 189)

With Baudrillard, then, we are not in the presence of a romantic. Quite the contrary. Here we are faced with a theorist who seeks to find a provocative objectivism. Invariably it is the woman, nonetheless, who is blinded or who dies in the silence of the effacement of metaphor. What kind of exchange is this? In an interview, Baudrillard was asked about his other infamous provocation: that as the American desert was so magnificent it might be appropriate to sacrifice a woman to celebrate it. His initially provocative words were: 'Death valley is as big and mysterious as ever. Fire heat, light: all the elements of sacrifice are here ... if something has to disappear, something matching the desert for beauty, why not a woman?' (A: 66). His response to the interviewer who asked 'what is the point of such a gratuitously provocative statement?' was to acknowledge the value of sacrifice: 'there is a certain amount of reciprocal sacrifice in seduction for instance. Something has to die ... perhaps desire or love must die' (BL: 153). This response is diverted directly into the metaphorical, yet he continues his answer by saying 'sacrificing a woman in the desert is a logical operation because in the desert one loses one's identity'. This begins to derive male identity from woman as radical other, as if to give a woman as gift would be a way of regaining the identity of the giver as a man. But then the response continues in the provocative mode: 'making a woman the object of the sacrifice is perhaps the greatest compliment I could pay her'. Baudrillard's answer then is made up of a number of very disparate elements which tend to contradict one another. There is continual movement from the literal to myth, there is a movement from the subject to the object, and a movement along the chain of the gift, from the subject to the recipient (Death Valley), and back to the subject and then to the object (woman) who is paid the 'compliment' by dint of an impossible exchange.

All these examples, which Baudrillard himself tends to accumulate and to compare and group together, are certainly very different in structure. For example, when he talks of the fatal strategy which emanates from the object as opposed to the banal strategy of the subject, and says that cruelty is characteristic of the object, some strange elisions of analysis are involved. There is a kind of cruel logic of the woman as object who donates her eye insofar as this subverts the position of the man. For Morris, this works only on condition that the woman's action is dematerialised, that is, becomes metaphor. But Baudrillard wants to insist that it is only a cruel fact in the effacement of metaphor, and cruel then to the subject (the man). On the other hand, Baudrillard wants to include the sentimental cannibalism and sacrifice also as instances of the cruelty of the object. It is extremely difficult to understand how this can be so: they appear transparently as the banal and cruel strategy of the subject transfigured into significant metaphor only through language. It is quite the reverse, therefore, of the process described by Baudrillard. In the case of the sacrifice in the desert, Baudrillard expresses its values in terms of loss to the subject (loss of identity). It is tortuous indeed to see this as the action of the cruel desert. In the case of the other victim, the Dutch girl, no evidence whatsoever is given even of this possibility, since she is mysteriously consumed as an amorous act, unless being a beautiful young girl is itself an offence to the subject. When Baudrillard describes the action of the Japanese cannibal as passing directly from metaphor to its effacement, it is only realised against the pure silence of the dead object. Even this is not strictly true since Baudrillard reports that the sound of a gun shot and the fall of the body were recorded on tape. Although the murder seems to have something of the air of ritual and sacrifice, this, like his other sacrificial images, is purely an artifice. They possess something of the characteristics of fateful events, but not the essential characteristics of rituals themselves.

Baudrillard's arguments are designed to provoke and to offend democratic sentiments as well as humanist ones. But here, too, many of his examples run into difficulties. In the interview, for example, he says 'seduction is not just a sexual strategy and it is not one-sided ... Both sides are deeply involved and the stakes are high.' He stresses that 'it is a very physical game and one of equality' (BL: 153). This is consistent with his emphasis on the nature of seduction as a play of challenge and response, and of reversibility of position, of metamorphosis of role, even of being. But even though this means an equality in the game in one sense, since initiatives can be reversed, he also says that 'it is almost an ideology played out to the detriment of democracy' (BL: 154). This implies that somewhere or other there is a formal equality. Baudrillard flirts with different images. One is that the male and female are like two different species: the 'model of amorous seduction, which also pursues the strangeness of the other sex, and the possibility of being initiated into it as into a different animal or vegetable species' (EC: 46). But elsewhere Baudrillard spells out his idea that it is man who wants to be initiated into woman but woman only wants to be metamorphosed into herself ... 'apparently they don't dream of being men ... They aren't devoured by curiosity for the other sex, rather they swoon away into their own ... ' This idea is expressed in the most forceful manner: women in their very narcissism express towards themselves affection and scrupulous attention to detail so that they become a pure event, and they metamorphose into themselves continually. What is left for men, he queries, but to search through women this power of metamorphosis? (FS: 185–6).

Feminist critics have been quick to point out that there is here the basis for Baudrillard's apparent equivocation on sexual difference. At one level, of course, a game in which initiatives can pass is one in which there is a degree of equality. But now Baudrillard has revealed that in this game the positions of the players have a basic structural inequality. As he expresses it, in this game the women are superior, but their superiority is not that of domination. It is related to the fact that their form of metamorphosis is inward (or shall we say that for Baudrillard this is their best option and what indeed defines women?). On the other hand, man wishes to cross from one species to the other, indeed to be initiated into the other species, and presumably to make the return journey. The 'drama', then, is on the side of the 'masculine'. The 'charm', however, is on the side of the feminine. Even though Baudrillard constructs notions of reversibility on both sides, obviously the 'reversibility' of the feminine is trapped and remains within the feminine as radical alterity.

He thus asserts the strategic equality of the sexes in seduction while insisting on a structural or positional asymmetry. And when feminists attempt to attack the inequality of positions, his response is to say: 'I am not in agreement with hard line feminist ideology which says that a woman as seducer is a degrading role. In my view the strategy of seduction is a happy, liberating power for women ... Unfortunately in feminism everything that happens to be female is defended, *l'écriture féminine*, poetry, and any kind of artistic creation, and this makes it a kind of mirror of masculine simulation. This is a negative simulation, an unfortunate simulation' (BL: 154). In the examples he provides here it does seem as if he believes women are just not made for artistic creativity of any kind. Modern feminism induces a new bad simulation, just as Marxism provides in its way a bad simulation of capitalism. Where can this argument lead except to nostalgia? Contrary to his claims that his position is not reactionary or nostalgic, it certainly appears backward looking: 'Men and women should not oppose each other. I believe one can regain feminine seductiveness as a positive virtue ... But of course I risk being misunderstood' (BL: 154). Clearly his use of the word 'regain' implies recovery of a lost situation, so why should he want to deny that his ideas are reactionary?

Masculinity

At this point it may be instructive to place Baudrillard in the context of French male theorising on gender. For my present purposes I have chosen to make the comparison between the founder of sociology, Auguste Comte, and Baudrillard, who announced the end of the social. There is no direct link between Comte and Baudrillard, but there are certainly some curious parallels between their theoretical systems. Baudrillard seems to invert many of the basic Comtean propositions, not least in his declarations concerning the end of the social and, with it, the end of sociology. Most notable, however, is the major shift in Baudrillard's work, which parallels one in Comte, from his sociological investigations into the nature of consumer society, written during an early Marxist period, to his critique of modern society from the more radical, more primitive position of symbolic fatalism. In this new position dating from the mid 1970s, Baudrillard's works elaborated a theory of fetishism at the heart of a modern society afflicted by new pathological forms. Baudrillard declares that 'Theory does not derive its legitimacy from established facts, but from future events. Its value is not in the past events it can illuminate, but in the shockwave of the events it prefigures' (CM: 215). This has a decidedly Comtean ring to it.

Baudrillard's general theory is articulated around the opposition between symbolic and semiotic cultures. The symbolic orders are, in principle, the equivalent of what Comte called theological stages of fetishism, through polytheism to monotheism. The semiotic orders and 'orders of simulation' follow a trajectory which is strictly parallel to stages defined within Comte's account of the rise of positivism and reason within the 'metaphysical' stage. If in Comte's later work fetishism reappears as a valuable potent force in the new social cult, in Baudrillard fetishism is more complex: on the one hand there is a fundamental role for the fatal, conceived actively in terms of fatal strategies, which exist in all human cultures, but on the other, very specifically connected with technology, fetishism is also powerfully theorised as the active pole within the advanced cultures. Baudrillard stigmatises the modern state, its democratic ideologies and human rights movements, in the same way as Comte (and Nietzsche): as essentially metaphysical and embroiled in self-contradictory forms of *ressentiment*. Whereas Comte after 1848 conceived the future as a linear and programmable procession in Euclidean time, Baudrillard maintains the primacy of precessive apocalyptic messianism in non-Euclidean mode. The paradox, he argues, is that the time of the world today as we encounter it in linearity, seems to want to hurry, seems to have a 'secret millenarianism about it' (IE: 9). Historical time, he says, entails the belief that there is a 'succession of non-meaningless facts, each engendering each other by cause and effect, but doing so without any absolute necessity and all standing open to the future, unevenly poised' (IE: 7). In effect this modern experience was not easily adopted, for 'this model of linearity must have seemed entirely fictitious, wholly absurd and abstract to cultures which had no sense of a deferred day of reckoning ... it was, indeed, a scenario which had some difficulty in establishing itself ... was not achieved without violence' (IE: 7). Yet this experience of time is that of both Comte and Marx as they moved beyond the immediacy of revolution: they tried to programme the transition to the higher social state.

Against Comte's programmed utopia, then, Baudrillard offers a (dys)utopian symbolic strategy of radical illusion. But it does have curious features as it always adjusts itself to the rules of the current game. His theory suggests as part of its very primitive form the primacy of a fatal feminine principle, that of seduction which prevails over all alternatives: virtue, truth, production, reality. In this respect, Baudrillard's strategy provides something of an updated inversion of Comte's law of the three states – fetishism is always predominant. His idea of the destiny of seduction suggests there are again but three logics: rituality, sociality, and digitality. Whereas Comte saw the triumph of science as marking the transition to a higher form of social legitimation, Baudrillard suggests that:

> Relative to the dangers of seduction that haunt the universe of games and rituals, our own sociality and the forms of communication and exchange it institutes, appear in direct proportion to their secularisation under the sign of the Law, as extremely impoverished, banal and abstract. But this is still only an intermediary state, for the age of the law has passed, and with it that of the socius and the social contract. Not only are we no longer living in an era of rules and rituals, we are no longer living in an era of laws and contracts. We live today according to Norms and Models, and we do not even have a term to designate that which is replacing sociality and the social. (S: 155)

Such a position inevitably follows Comte's anti-feminism by a rejection of modern second-wave feminism as a phenomenon of contemporary *ressentiment* and metaphysics. It also stigmatises modern feminism as falling under a form of gender identification where femininity becomes a mode of semiotic production, this time of the eroticised material body requiring sexual performance as an obligatory end. Thus sexual liberation and emancipation lead not to a reconstruction of the social contract, a new dialectic, or a religious bond – as envisaged at the beginning of sociology by the Saint-Simonians – but to a logic of excess. This logic is one which attacks and breaks down the traditional polarities of ritual exchange, and produces what Baudrillard calls a new transpolitical form, the transsexual (TE: 20f.); and one of the crucial sites of such a process is the culture of male–female symbolic exchanges. The modern crisis is not one simply of the female role and identity (as had been widely believed in sociology since the 1950s): the movement of sexual liberation attacks traditional forms of masculinity as well, transforming the modalities of seduction (they are complicit products of masculine desire: positive and judged by performance).

It is possible now to situate Baudrillard's position in terms of some modern French variations of the ways in which past futures have been cast as utopian or dystopian states. These visions could, charitably, be viewed as theoretical devices, ideal types, whose main purposes were or are to provide means of analysing current problems, particularly where the individual theorist has immense difficulty in living within them. More than one such theorist has said, following Auguste Comte, 'I live posthumously'. The modality is quite different from the dilemmas opened by Foucault: we find in his work a complete refusal to indulge in utopian thought and general programmes, but at the same time there is an engagement in radical sexual experimentation, a desire to make unambiguous discoveries within the sexual experience (discussed in Halperin 1995). In the messianic frames there is, however, an ambivalence, even a tension, between the future as the terminus of a current trend or tendency, and the future seen as a leap into a new condition. French theory today is increasingly taken up with Walter Benjamin's distinction between future as programmed utopia, and future as explosive or implosive catastrophic shifts (see Benjamin 1970: 255–66). There is an alternative, one might even say a third, way: negative utopianism. Derrida's position holds that the messianic frame is essential to the Western historical experience of justice, but what must never happen is the arrival of the messiah, a parody of the 'wait' for the female messiah inaugurated by the Saint-Simonians in the 1830s (see the discussion and documents in Moses et al. 1993). The ultimately disillusioned position, that of Baudrillard, holds that the day of judgement came, but the messiah missed the appointment. One might note that we find in the variations of Derrida and Baudrillard the Jewish and Catholic patriarchal forms under threat, retrenched, partially reconstructed in a Nietzschean direction.[1] Anything more radical would, it seems, have to be a revolution at the level of the matrix, and this is not on the agenda. The revolution is behind us, and it did not end in transcendence but in liberation.

Baudrillard's writings are however somewhat more complex than the disillusioned formula of messianic parapraxis might suggest. The history of masculinity, he suggests, runs as follows: at the beginning of the nineteenth century – the opening of the crisis of masculinity – there was a replacement of aristocratic forms of seduction by a new (bourgeois) form of romantic love. This new configuration projected a specific ideal model of femininity on to women, or one might say the femininity of the new woman was 'called' into existence by men experiencing a crisis of alienation in their masculinity, their own sexual ambivalence. Politically, feminism also answered to a call from men for a new woman as citizen. Second-wave feminism is the more recent product of the male demand for sexual woman who is also both citizen and intellectual. But all of these progressive changes have had the effect of breaking down the symbolic structures of radical otherness in the culture between men and women. This is a demand for a sex 'removed from artifice, illusion and seduction' and recreated within a structure of sexual (in)difference. It is at this point that the initiative has passed to women, but ironically for Baudrillard not to woman as fatal object:

> We have here the problem of a woman, having once become the subject of desire, no longer finding the other she could desire as such ... For the secret never lies in the equivalent exchange of desires, under the sign of egalitarian difference; it lies in inventing the other who will be able to play on – and make sport of – my own desire, defer it, and thus arouse it indefinitely. Is the female gender capable today of producing – since it no longer wishes to personify it – this same seductive otherness? Is the female gender still hysterical enough to invent the other? (PC: 120)

Now in a crucial sense this is another post-messianic problem posed in Baudrillard's recent writing. Not only is there a general scenario in which the (male) messiah missed his appointment with the day of judgement. There is another: the day of the historic reversal of power within gender relations.

Baudrillard's view here is that this appointment was not missed by parapraxis, but that the dominant invention is here born of *ressentiment*: the new male is produced by modern woman only as agent of sexual harassment. For Baudrillard this is also to miss the appointment, for 'it marks the arrival on the scene of an impotent, victim's sexuality, a sexuality impotent to constitute itself either as object or as subject of desire in its paranoid wish for identity and difference' (PC: 122). The call for the female messiah to appear was indeed answered, but in a way which fails to produce either a new masculinity or a new femininity. The new woman is equally impotent. Baudrillard's analysis of the pop star Madonna provides a picture of the female messiah who, even if she missed the appointment, did arrive:

> Madonna is 'desperately' fighting in a world where there is no response – the world of sexual indifference. Hence the urgent need for hypersexual sex, the signs of which are exacerbated precisely because they are no longer addressed to anyone ... For want of some other who would deliver her from herself, she is unrelentingly forced to provide her own sexual enticement, to build up for herself a panoply of accessories – in the event a sadistic panoply, from which she tries to wrench herself away. Harassment of the body by sex, harassment of the body by signs. (PC: 126)

Not only the sexual politics of harassment and *ressentiment* but, since there is no radical other to her identity, she becomes a woman who harasses her own body 'in a cycle or closed circuit'. It is in this sense that Madonna can 'play all the roles' and 'all the versions of sex' so as to 'exploit this fantastic absence of identity'.

It is easy to scorn these theories. Because Comtean sociology fell into ridicule, Durkheim built up modern French sociology on quite a different terrain, though it was profoundly anti-feminist. Baudrillard has deserted sociology on his own initiative and few mainstream French sociologists have regretted his departure. It seems clear that both Comte and Baudrillard found it difficult to come to terms with what they have regarded as a corrupt and depraved world. Comte sought a way out in a sentimental and optimistic world of sociological theory-fiction, saved by scientific knowledge and a providential fetishism. Baudrillard, terrified of making a naive judgement, chased fetishistic perversities in a downward 'spiral of the worst'. The judgements produced are those which offend and which are meant to offend a culture of democratic indifferentiation. Baudrillard's judgements have appeared notoriously sexist and misogynist. However, this strange variation on a Comtean theme points to a radical future for gender relations: the culture of sexual *ressentiment* and indifference (in all its transpolitical variants) is but a form of sexual (dis)illusion in which, paradoxically, a logic of hysterical excess is unleashed. Instead of moving to a reasonable consensus, events shoot off with great energy, hysterically, to extremes. Baudrillard's position refuses to admit the adequacy of a positivist or critical sociology of this situation. The role of fatal post-messianic theory-fiction is to challenge the world into existence, not to freeze it. Whereas Comte sought to challenge the world into the good through the programmed fantasy of an harmonic sexual utopia, Baudrillard challenges it into a fantastic genealogy of hyperspace encounters.

It could be argued that writers such as Comte and Baudrillard are marginal to current concerns in the field of gender studies. However, their approaches belong to a tradition which has always given gender a central position in its sociological analyses. But if both writers take the future state as a fundamental element in their analyses, they do so in two fundamentally different ways, different forms of messianicity. It is also clear that although Baudrillard's thought has evolved through Marxism, there are nonetheless common roots with Comte in the Saint-Simonian origins of social theory, and these share many common elements with the Western Judaeo-Christian messianic tradition itself. What distinguishes these writers is that they both sought, like Marx, to replace theological with positive futures. They both, however, also replaced the purely secular modes of social analysis with ones which combined fetishism/fatalism with positivism.

The assessment of these theories must take into account the fact that they are expressly utopian. Both develop critiques of democratic forms and reject the massification of modern societies. Both write in order to reveal the features of a catastrophic social development: Comte to save humanity from it, Baudrillard to alert humanity to its inevitability. Comte envisioned a humanity committed to chaste marriage and worship of the Virgin; Baudrillard envisages a humanity committed to internet pornography and the worship of Madonna. These are mirror images of each other, and are produced out of a common frame in which a stable set of gender positions allowed symbolic ritual exchanges, under traditional patriarchy, between men and women. Whether out of the effectiveness of the women's movements (comparatively weak in France) or through the structural social changes brought about in the modernisation process, these traditional patriarchal formations are threatened with catastrophic collapse.

CHAPTER 8

War

> The apocalypse of real time and pure war along with
> the triumph of the virtual over the real, are realised
> at the same time ... a sign that the space of the event
> has become hyperspace ... the undecidability created
> by the unleashing of the two opposed principles.
> Soft war and pure war go boating. (GWNP: 50)

Baudrillard and Virilio are often associated together as the pre-eminent French postmodern theorists (see Kroker 1992 and Ritzer 1997): writing for the same publications (on the French journal *Traverses*, for example, and in numerous Semiotext(e) publications); attending the same conferences (see for example *Looking Back on the End of the World* (Kamper & Wulf 1989)); interviewed for the same publication series: by Sylvère Lotringer for Semiotext(e) (see FF, BL and Virilio & Lotringer 1997), by Rotzer – a chapter each for Boer Verlag (Rotzer 1995), and at book length by Philippe Petit for Grasset (Virilio in *Cybermonde, La Politique du Pire* (1996), and Baudrillard in *Le Paroxyste indifferent*). The two writers refer to each other in friendly terms, but admit some profound differences. Virilio: 'I have a friendly relationship with Baudrillard, even if I don't always agree with him' (in Rotzer 1995: 98). Baudrillard: 'We have worked together ... without any problem ... His analysis of the cyberworld is intransigent, inexorable, fatal I might dare say, and I find it beautiful and remarkable ... [but he] puts himself in the position of the anti-apocalypse prophet, having been persuaded that the worst can come about. On this point we have ended up going our separate ways. I do not believe in his real apocalypse ... it is the coming of the virtual itself which is our apocalypse, and this deprives us of the real apocalypse' (P: 46–7). Virilio: 'There's a neonihilism in him that I don't like' (in Rotzer 1995: 98). Baudrillard: 'Virilio takes a position which is very clearly moral ... Ultimately his analysis is more radical than mine.'[1] These cryptic remarks refer in fact to something of a major divergence, and it is highly instructive to follow through the logic of this particular difference of opinion, particularly their different analyses of war.

1968

Baudrillard and Virilio were both at the University of Nanterre in 1968. Baudrillard lectured in sociology, and in 1968 saw his *The System of*

Objects into publication. Virilio, with the architect Claude Parent, was preparing to build a structure at the university called 'The Pendular Destabiliser', a purely experimental double oblique structure (rather like two bunkers joined together side by side in the form of an X) elevated twelve metres above the ground and isolated from the rest of the world: 'there was no telephone, no post, no means of communication – except for a little hole in the wall that we could talk to each other through' (Parent & Virilio 1996: 55). The events of May 1968 ended the experiment. Virilio joined the student occupation of the *Odéon*. Baudrillard made a rather obscure reference to this experiment in a passage in *For a Critique of the Political Economy of the Sign:* 'the functionality of an object ... in an oblique architecture is not to be useful or equilibrated, but to be oblique ... It is the coherence of the system that defines the aesthetic-functional value of the elements' (FCPES: 191). For Baudrillard, Virilio's experiment was simply an architectural variant of the object system.

Virilio soon abandoned oblique architecture. His new ideas emerge over the period 1969–75 in the journals *Esprit, Cause commune,* and *Critique,* essays which are collected together in *L'Insecurité du territoire* (Virilio 1993). Here he develops the idea of critical space out of the joy of having been able to sleep in a lecture theatre at the Sorbonne, breakfast in a box at the opera house, eat lunch in a director's office, find a nursery in the library, find a games room in the Renault showroom; indeed, of having been able to find France, its stations, airports, schools, shops, as a space to be occupied, thereby reversing the alienated state of everyday life (Ibid. 86–7): just as there is a need for freedom of speech, so there is also a need for freedom of movement. A barricade, he wrote, is not simply a territorial limit but a construction of a new kind of liberated space, a 'new mode of the appropriation of space and time' (Ibid. 89). Although Virilio uses the experience of May 1968, in these years, he does not adopt Marxist language or ideas (with the possible rare exception of an observation that his work concerns the primacy of a revolution in the 'means of destruction' rather than 'means of production' (Virilio & Lotringer 1997: 105)). What interests him is the experience of space in the changing character of the overall strategic situation in its military aspect, and increasingly the logic of mass communications which he sees as its inevitable counterpart. 'We're in a system in which military order dominates ... no matter if that order is socialist, capitalist or anything else' (Ibid. 96).

Virilio's reflections on the failure of May 1968 parallel those of Baudrillard in many respects. The leading elite of capitalist civilisation has become a 'jet set' which no longer resides in traditional and expected locations in time and space. This counter-revolution succeeds through an escalation to 'hyper-communication', transforming the terrain of struggle. Fundamental innovations and technical revolutions put an end to any hope of a genuine revolution in the oblique, or 'habitable circulation'. Indeed his former position, which depended on a critique of the stasis of bourgeois society is radically reversed. He charts the emergence of nuclear deterrence, 'total peace', not as stasis but as absolute war (Virilio 1993: 71). The old communism equated progress with speed, but speed is no longer the sign of progress: quite the opposite (Ibid. 266–70).

Speed

It is instructive at this point to compare Virilio's experience with that of Baudrillard, with whom he began to collaborate on the journal *Traverses* from 1976. Both Virilio and Baudrillard reversed their positions on the meaning of the events of May 1968, coming in the mid 1970s to a common view that the political situation had rendered untenable a simple commitment to revolution and progress. The points of departure were, however, very different. Baudrillard's background in literature, anthropology and sociology was in marked contrast with Virilio's background in craftwork, theology and military architecture. But the convergence was strong and condensed around the acceptance of a new social condition marked by the success of material consumerism and the dominance of mass communication in a condition of political stasis (theorised by Virilio as a paradoxical situation of pure war). There were, however, clear differences of opinion. As Virilio was later to remark (Virilio & Lotringer 1997: 125), Baudrillard's key text, *Symbolic Exchange and Death* developed no discussion of the war machine (for take up of this idea one has to go to Deleuze and Guattari); Baudrillard if anything moved to a pagan position of symbolic exchange, which saw the Christian forms adhered to by Virilio as the very source of modern simulacra. And while Virilio sought a base in the social for retrenchment of resistance to ongoing technological transformations, Baudrillard notoriously announced the 'end of the social'. Baudrillard's essay on the architecture of the Pompidou Centre (*L'Effet Beaubourg: implosion et dissuasion* (in SS)) stands in remarkable contrast with Virilio's *Bunker Archeology* (1975). Just as Virilio had described the bunker as a dead animal, so Baudrillard began his essay on the Beaubourg by defining it as a 'carcass of flux and signs' (SS: 61) and 'an imperial compression – figure of a culture already crushed by its own weight – like moving automobiles suddenly frozen in a geometric solid' (SS: 63). Instead of celebrating the idea of polyvalent space in the interior of the new building, Baudrillard is scathing in his contempt for the idea of 'circulation' in this space, with its 'immense to-and-fro movement similar to that of suburban commuters'. The paradox, he said, is that people search for a 'corner which is precisely not one, [and so] exhaust themselves secreting an artificial solitude ... the ideology of visibility, transparency, of polyvalency' (SS: 62). It leads Baudrillard to a famous formulation: from now on the vision of a possible revolutionary explosion has to be replaced by that of an implosion; and the same is true of the city itself: 'fires, war, revolutions, criminal marginality, catastrophes: the whole problematic of the anticity, of the negativity internal or external to the city, has some archaic relation to its true mode of annihilation' (SS: 70–1). Baudrillard reflects that the events of 1968 have to be rethought: 'something else began ... the violent involution of the social' (SS: 73).

Virilio's problematic in the mid 1970s shifts from space to time, and from an expansive politics of mobilisation and liberalisation, to a defensive and conservative politics of resistance to acceleration and against Baudrillard to a defence of the social. *Speed and Politics* ((1977)1986), and *Popular Defense and Ecological Struggles* ((1978) 1990) register the scope of the vast change in Virilio's position. Responding to the appeals of theologians like Bonhoeffer, Virilio begins to warn of the dangers implied in the new state of the world, dangers to the experience of space, of the city, of democracy; and of the new possibility of apocalypse brought about by technologies and strategies newly available to and adopted by the military elite. In a sense the essay *Speed and Politics*, with its theory of power through control of movement, a 'dromocracy' (Virilio 1986: 70), was the culmination of an analysis applicable to a world already passing away. If the proletariat still thinks in terms of the control of streets and physical movement (Ibid. 103), the military thinks otherwise: it thinks logistically in relation to new meeting points such as airports and highways, and telecommunications (Ibid. 104). Communism died, fascism survives (Ibid. 117) and has adapted. In this new world, where information is immediately available through instantaneous communications, a permanent state of emergency is created: 'The violence of speed has become both the violence and the law, the word's destiny and its destination' (Ibid. 151).

Virilio draws out these conclusions more dramatically in *Popular Defense and Ecological Struggles*: 'If ... civilians could have resisted the assault of the war machine, gotten ahead of it, by creating a defense without a body, condensed nowhere, it is quite evident that today they don't even realise that technology has surpassed this kind of defense' (Virilio 1990: 71). This is because there is ' ... no need for an armed body to attack civilians, so long as the latter have been properly trained to turn on their radios or plug in their television sets' (Ibid.). In these conditions the political state declines, and where 'hyper-communicability' exists there grows totalitarian power (Ibid. 64–6). The right of armed defence by citizens is lost, while on the other hand 'from now on' the military power is so 'shapeless' it can no longer be identified as it installs itself in a regime of generalised security: an important and irreversible shift from a state of political and civil justice to a state of logistical and military discipline (Ibid. 75). This is achieved through the systematic destruction of all the major forms of social solidarity which previously offered real resistance to the state: particularly the family, conceived by Virilio as essentially a combat unit. The liberation of women effectively weakens the solidarity of the family as a defensive form against the state. The resort to terrorism by ultra-left-wing groups again only serves to strengthen, not weaken, the war machine (Ibid. 88). This creates a paradox: the possibility that the revolution can succeed through control of the streets has been lost yet 'there is no more revolution except in resistance' (Virilio 1986: 82).

Baudrillard's position in the mid 1970s does not aim to find resistance in the social, but to pit 'culture', in the anthropological sense, against the new regimes of simulacra. Baudrillard's critical essays only work on the basis that he can say what this opposition between them is. 'Culture' at this moment in his thought is an ordered structure, 'a site of the secret, of seduction, of initiation, of a restrained and highly ritualized symbolic exchange' (SS: 64). While the Beaubourg Centre is 'nothing but a huge effort to transmute [the] famous traditional culture of meaning into the aleatory order of signs, into an order of simulacra [the third] that is completely homogeneous with the flux and pipes of the facade' (SS: 65). It is interesting to note that in a recent interview Virilio, rejecting his 1968 position and now in agreement with Baudrillard, remarked that the Beaubourg was 'already a symptom of the mobilisation of architecture' in a way which paralleled the acceleration of the real (Virilio & Brausch 1997: 74).

Baudrillard's analysis here developed as part of his theory of 'orders of simulacra' (SED, part 2), a topic taken up as the feature of a special issue of the journal *Traverses* (No. 10, *Le Simulacra*) in February 1978. Baudrillard's contribution was the essay '*La Precession des simulacres*' (Baudrillard 1978: 3–37; SS:1–42), and Virilio wrote '*La Dromoscopie ou l'ivresse des grandeurs*' (Virilio 1978: 65–72) which was also published in an expanded version in the journal *Critique* (vol. 34: 324–37, as '*La Dromoscopie ou la lumière de la vitesse*', this version reproduced as Chapter 6 of *L'Horizon négatif* (Virilio 1984: 143–55). It is not surprising to find that Virilio's discussion starts with the statement that 'movement commands the event' (Ibid. 143), which we find later is derived from Napoleon (Ibid. 161). Virilio's idea sees simulacra as phenomena closely linked to those of command posts, control consoles, cockpits. He develops the idea that with moving vehicles like cars, the travellers see the world in a new way, a double reduction: of the time-distance of the voyage and the new screen vision of the world. He calls this the dromoscopic simulation (Ibid. 146). Thus Virilio's idea of simulation is quite different from that of Baudrillard and closer to that of McLuhan (who theorised about the new vision of the world produced by the speed of trains). Virilio's thesis is that the driver in such a position of simulation in the dromocratic order maintains the dictatorship of movement (Ibid. 148). Virilio traces the idea of the 'conductors' of peoples behind the 'dromoscopic screen of absolute power', before passing to the motorcyclist and 'conductors of families who reproduce in their little everyday movements (*évasions*) the dromocratic order of great invasions'(Ibid. 154–5). The discussion suggests that now it is the earth itself which is the vehicle, and all perception of the movement of the sun, moon and stars is equivalent to perception of 'the real' through a panoramic screen (Ibid. 159). The way is open for new means of teleguidance or what he calls 'dromovisual apparatuses' (Ibid. 160). But against McLuhan he argues that the significant developments here cannot adequately be seen as or reduced to the technological; the crucial effects concern the new levels of rapidity of communication between interlocutors: the violence of speed is not a simple technological phenomenon. Here the motor has been war, with industrial civilisation its transformed effect, and the new acceleration producing the condition of pure war (Ibid. 161).

Virilio's 'simulations' are representations of the real world, representations which are substituted for one another as technology develops. Baudrillard's conception of these relations is more complex: the real is not a brute given, but an historically and socially evolved form of appropriation of the world (and replaces other forms through their constant and systematic destruction). For Baudrillard, then, representation 'stems from the principle of the equivalence of the sign and the real', whereas simulation, 'on the contrary, stems ... from the radical negation of the sign as value, from the sign as reversion ... of every reference'. In this new situation 'there is no longer a Last Judgement to separate the false from the true' (SS: 6). As he had noted in his essay on the Pompidou Centre in Paris, the 'Beaubourg illustrates very well that an order of simulacra only establishes itself on the alibi of the previous order' (SS: 64). What separates Baudrillard and Virilio at this point in time is not just Christianity (where Baudrillard takes a Nietzschean position which is anathema to Virilio (Virilio & Lotringer 1997: 133), but essentially a dispute about the theory of the real as a referent for simulation, and particularly the social as referent. The different emphasis given by Virilio to the theory of war could be seen as providing a relatively specialised zone which ensures that theoretical topics do not come into direct contact, but which allows theoretical exchanges between them to occur.

Both Virilio and Baudrillard follow McLuhan in their own way: the medium is the message. The development of the mass media, tele-technologies, brings about the ecstasy of communication and the hegemony of the screen, the vision machine. As I have noted, Virilio made this transition in his writings over the period 1969–75 (in *L'Insécurité du territoire*) with his thesis that acceleration is generalised through communication. This becomes a decisive new step in his account of dromocracy: at the end of *Speed and Politics* Virilio concludes with the observation that with the advent of nuclear war and the new means of communication 'the war-machine becomes (thanks to the reflexes of the strategic calculator) the very decision for war' (Virilio (1977) 1986: 139–40). Preparation for war is part of war itself, and creates 'extreme proximity of parties in which the immediacy of information immediately creates the crisis' (Ibid. 143). Virilio suggests that this realises what was most feared by Clausewitz, the 'full discharge' of total war (Ibid. 151). The Red Brigades in Italy in February 1978 called for all militants to 'act militarily in order to act politically against the "bunkers in which the agents of counter-revolution hide"' (Virilio 1990: 42). Virilio, stung to reply, wrote a resolute critique of this aim: it is too late for any assault, only popular defence is possible. But it is clear this creates a crisis at the heart of Virilio's position: there are three kinds of resistance – first, to struggle against the war-machine by declaring war on it; secondly, to enter its body and divert its effect; and third, simply to act defensively where possible forms of solidarity arise and to build up these solidarities where possible. The former seemed outmoded by the 1970s, but the question which haunts Virilio's project of popular resistance is what forms would it take and are they effective? Even more pressing is the question of what happened to the work of transforming the technological developments brought about by the military machine?

The Gulf War

When pure war changed gear and the Gulf War broke out in 1991, Virilio, just like Baudrillard, was keen to locate and analyse its new logic, in the light of 25 years of theorising. Virilio's analysis, in *L'Écran du desert* (Virilio 1991b) concluded that a shift had indeed taken place and that this was the first 'post-modern war' (Ibid. 177) in the sense that it was now clear, as had been foreseen, that many of the temporal and spatial aspects of war had been completely transformed by communication and other technologies (see the commentary on this transition in Bogard 1996: 78–97). This war, where the military vision machine proved itself sovereign, was for Virilio a world war 'in miniature', and deserved to be known as World War III 'in reduction' (Virilio 1991b: 162). The instantaneity of decision-making, using information produced at an unprecedented speed, meant that space-time relations were fused in a total 'electromagnetic environment' (Ibid. 165). Much has been made of the apparent difference between Baudrillard and Virilio on the Gulf War; indeed, the difference appeared sharp at the time. Yet Virilio introduced the spectre of the 'fourth front': the speed of communication is so rapid and decisive it rules out at a stroke effective responsibility and democratic control. It creates the paradoxical elimination of the distinction between true and false, the fusion of object and image, even of defence and attack (Ibid. 182). And Baudrillard wrote at the time: 'in confronting our opinions on the war with the diametrically opposed opinions of Paul Virilio, one of us betting on apocalyptic escalation and the other on deterrence and the indefinite virtuality of war, we concluded that this decidedly strange war went in both directions at once' (GWNP: 49).

But this conclusion is superficial. For Baudrillard the crucial point was that the separation between war and peace was dissolved into virtual transpolitical forms. Virilio, on the other hand, requires that the two remain separate in order to perform his critique. We can say therefore that Virilio noted something Baudrillard did not: a new situation of the bunker. Unlike the bunkers on the Atlantic Wall, Saddam's bunkers were hidden and disguised, resembling other 'furtive' phenomena of this new type of war (Virilio 1991b: 119). These bunkers were hidden in the desert, a modern Atlantis. Thus Virilio, from a Baudrillardian point of view, seems to have taken at face value the war machine's own propaganda (see Keeble 1997: 166–87, esp. p. 180); a further reversal had taken place. The destructive arms were now exposed, but the defensive infrastructures were disguised (Virilio 1991b: 121). The new bunkers were proof against nuclear attack and designed to maintain hundreds of soldiers in a new kind of hostile environment with sophisticated air filtration systems (Ibid. 121). On the other hand, one of the great 'errors' of the allies was to have bombed a civilian bunker less well disguised than others (Ibid. 189, 185–6), compounded paradoxically by the problem of an inability to assess accurately the effect of its attacks even with the immense panoply of sophisticated spying apparatuses. These seemed to be able to give precise information about position only, but to be unable to play any significant qualitative role in the verification of damage inflicted.

Curiously, however, despite Baudrillard's apparent argument that these wars did not take place, something nevertheless did occur. At the end of Baudrillard's articles on the Gulf War, he reflected that the war's 'decisive stake' had been

> the consensual reduction of Islam to the global order. Not to destroy it but to domesticate it ... and the symbolic challenge that Islam represents for the entire West ... This was how it happened in the Vietnam War: the day when China was neutralised, when the 'wild' Vietnam ... was replaced by a truly bureaucratic ... organisation ... the war stopped immediately. Same thing with the Algerian War: its end, which was believed to be impossible, took place of its own accord ... (GWNP: 85)

Baudrillard's writings on the Bosnian crisis have continued this line of reasoning:

> The short of it is that we will bomb a few Serb positions with smoke-mortars, but we will never really intervene against them, since their work is basically our own ... In the event of a powerful Muslim offensive the international forces will suddenly become efficient. (In Cushman & Mestrovic 1996: 85)

So there is a remarkable thematic continuation in Baudrillard's analyses of war throughout this period: while he locates the real process as one of annihilation of any symbolic challenge to the West, he also argues somewhat paradoxically that war itself is no longer possible: 'We prefer the exile of the virtual, of which television is the universal mirror, to the catastrophe of the real' (GWNP: 28). This phrase was published just as the war itself broke out in the air and on the ground. Baudrillard asked: 'The Gulf War: is it really taking place?' (GWNP: 29ff.). His response was that the existence of war was undecidable:

> What is most extraordinary is that the two hypotheses, the apocalypse of real time ... along with the triumph of the virtual over the real, are realised at the same time, in the same space-time, each in implacable pursuit of the other. It is a sign that the space of the event has become hyperspace ... (Ibid. 50).

What is curious in Baudrillard's writing at this point is that there is very little third-order simulacral theorising about the role of the media and the shift into virtual-reality war.

The argument is developed in terms of the process of deterrence and the secret system of complicities between the adversaries implicated in the apparent conflict. So Baudrillard's thesis is that this war was an event of a quite new type:

> Eastern Europe saw the collapse of communism, the construction of which had indeed been an historic event, borne by a vision of the world and a utopia. By contrast, its collapse is borne by nothing and bears nothing, but only opens onto a confused desert ... (Ibid. 70).

This thesis, along with those concerning such events as the collapse of the Algerian revolution, is in many respects a quite conventional sociological thesis relating to the realities of the world below the official pronouncements of politicians. And these theses do not in any sense propose a simple abandonment of the idea of the real and the category of reality; indeed, they depend on the difference between the real and the war as simulation. The new situation is brought into existence by a very specific conjunction of forces. Here the facts of cold war, deterrence, and particularly the collapse of revolutionary movements on the ground or through bureaucratic subversion (China, Vietnam, Algeria), effectively change the character of war. The war also becomes a different kind of war, a different phenomenon: the intervention of the new technologies of the virtualisation of war made these wars paradoxical. In the terminology he has developed for fourth-order simulacra, they become graspable only as singularities in hyperspace.

Baudrillard against Virilio

It is clear that Baudrillard and Virilio now work in different theoretical frames. Virilio never ceases to insist that his own position makes war dangerous but also productive – 'war and not commerce is the source of the city' – something most are unwilling to accept (Virilio & Lotringer 1997: 30). Thus we must be clear: war and peace are not simply opposite states. They do not figure as unique categories, but are transformed into each other: the priest transforms war into peace, the warrior transforms peace into war. Virilio models himself, however, not on a Christian example, but on a pagan one: the Greeks brought politics and citizenship into existence out of war. In the *agon* the individual dies for the city. He exchanges this death for a new life. But in the new situation the 'military man is a false priest because the question of death doesn't interest him. He's an executioner, not a priest. A new inquisitor' (Ibid. 1997: 49).

Virilio, in his own way, is also fascinated by the emergence of a new type of inertial mode of being, exemplified by Howard Hughes, who 'ended up a technological monk in the desert of Las Vegas, without getting out of bed' (Ibid. 73). All he did was to watch films. He saw *Ice Station Zebra* 164 times: 'he never stopped watching a film that represented exactly that same inertia in a polar city ... ' (Ibid.). 'What fascinated me about Howard Hughes ... was the fact that he managed to foreshadow a mass situation' (Ibid. 74). But Virilio asks: 'Who are these people fascinated by their electronic windows?' This interests him since here 'we have a phenomenon of inertia and death on the spot ... a sedentariness in dead time' (Ibid.). The earnest and humourless logic of Virilio's position makes it quite different therefore from that of Baudrillard. Virilio in essence has a theory of the relentless and accumulative dromocracy, while if Baudrillard's 'orders of simulacra' appear accumulative (since they abolish previous orders), in the end they occupy a complex space-time and are subject to reversibility, for the last judgement has already occurred ('might it not perhaps be necessary to replace Paul Virilio's dromology with a palindromology?', asks Baudrillard wickedly (IE: 122)). Virilio tries to specify a 'grey ecology': a new kind of resistance (it has no means) to a new pollution (it is 'omnipolitan' (Virilio 1997: 143)). For Baudrillard, Virilio's 'attempt to escape the apocalypse of the virtual, is ... the last of our utopian desires' (IE: 117).

Virilio now outlines his strategy: 'Proximity, the single interface between all bodies, all places, all points of the world – that's the tendency. And I push this tendency to extremes. It's not science fiction. Science and technology develop the unknown, not knowledge. Science develops what is not rational. That's what fiction is' (Virilio & Lotringer 1997: 62). To pass from fiction into the 'real', however, requires another step. He is profoundly furtive about his capabilities

on this front: 'I have no solution to offer'; and he adds: 'if there's a
salvation it lies in the humility of philosophical, scientific and political
thinking ... a radical scientific and philosophical humility. We are
nothing' (in Rotzer 1995: 103–4).

Baudrillard's position is quite different. On the one hand it has a
content: the resistance that comes from the genuine symbolic cultures;
he seeks to find and locate the internal points of extreme modernity
where the linearity, exchange, accumulation, break down. As with his
writings on aesthetics (bad simulation), on sexual politics (unfortunate
simulation), there is here, on the terrain of war, the bad simulation of
resistance offered by Saddam Hussein and others – actually a crucial
complicity. But this thesis is now argued in terms of the hyperreality
of war, not in linear space-time, but in paradoxical space-time. So
Baudrillard's thesis also has quite a different form from that of Virilio.
It does not rest on a defence of the real but on the theoretical divide
between the symbolic and the semiotic cultures: 'Otherness is of the
order of the incomparable. It is not exchangeable in terms of a
general equivalent, it is not negotiable, and yet it circulates in the
mode of complicity and the dual relation, both in seduction and in
war' (PC: 122).

CHAPTER 9

Art and Photography

> Bringing out [the] analytical truth of the object, the
> world and the social sphere, by deconstructing their
> appearances is the aesthetic and political move of
> modernity. Now, it is precisely the opposite which
> needs to be done ... (FCM: 115)

In Baudrillard's first period it was art, and later photography, which
were the privileged, even exemplary, sites of illustration of his basic
theses on the rise and fall of representations. If music is sometimes
alluded to it is clearly not one of his central concerns (BL: 24).
Literature and writing are crucially important to Baudrillard but are
rarely, with the exception of a short note on science fiction writing
(SS: 121–7), accorded the organised and genealogical analysis that is
given to art. It is not only in his essays and poetry but also in his writing
on art and photography that Baudrillard develops both theory and a
detailed working out of his ideas into practice. In this chapter I first
present the analytic schema, and then go on to examine his ideas on
and practice of art and photography.

Genealogy

Sometimes a translation can create problems in understanding
Baudrillard's position. One example is the misleading implication
of this rendering: ' ... this dimension, that of perspective, is also still
the bad faith of the sign in relation to reality. And because of bad
faith, all art since the Renaissance has been rot' (in Baudrillard 1988d:
157). Baudrillard was not a little taken aback when confronted with
this translation: 'I am not against art, so you exaggerate a bit when
you use the word "antipathy". I am like everyone else. There are
things about European art that I admire as much as anyone else'
(BL: 24). Another more recent translation of the same passage reads
' ... this dimension, that of perspective, always indicates the bad
conscience of the sign relative to reality – a bad conscience that had
eaten away at all painting since the Renaissance' (S: 64). It is now
becoming possible to chart Baudrillard's general assessment of art
since the Renaissance, though there is no single systematic exposition
to work from.

Baudrillard's conception of the evolution of art into modernity was outlined in three remarkable chapters of *For a Critique of the Political Economy of the Sign* (FCPES: chs 4, 5, 10). Already there the basic opposition is outlined between symbolic cultures and semiotic orders. But the idea of the symbolic is, at this moment, related to Michel Foucault's analysis of the pre-modern notion of the 'prose of the world' (Foucault 1970: 34–5; cited in FCPES: 103). Baudrillard elaborates on Foucault's conception and follows the emergence of the modern system through a genealogy of the signature. In the pre-modern cultural system, language is thought to be a part of, to be in the world. The 'signature of the world' is written directly on things. It is God's hand, to be read and recognised. It is the expression of the world's essential meaning, there is no question of its possible inauthenticity. The world is transcendent and contains language within itself, so art is only a description of the world which is already in the world. The original authorship is the creation of the world. In this culture the work of art is a more or less adequate copy of the already given signature of the world. The individual painting is not an object. It only becomes an art object when the signature, written by the artist himself, is part of the nature of the work. Modern art stamps the signature of the individual artist on the representation. This makes forgery possible along with all the other forms of inauthenticity and the differences between them.

Up to the Renaissance, *episteme* (as defined by Foucault) is the divinely authored order of the world, which has undisputed precedence. Baudrillard takes off from this idea and suggests that after this point it is the work of the named artist which assumes precedence, and the artist's signature which now guarantees the work's authenticity (FCPES: 104). From this point the very practice of painting changes. No longer can the work result from the cooperation of a team of artists. The work, like language, becomes separated from the world, indeed there is no longer a 'prose of the world'. Foucault noted that it is from this point that the games of chimera and *trompe l'oeil*, games of illusion, begin (Foucault 1970: 51). From now on, Baudrillard argues, following this line of thought, the signature determines the meaning of the work, since it is 'fundamentally homogeneous with the combinatory order of signs which is that of the painting'. Indeed, later in the evolution of Western art, it becomes possible to imagine a painting which is 'only a signature' (FCPES: 105). The modern art system hinges on the signature, which is

> a sign different from other signs in the painting, but homogeneous with them; a name different from the names of other paintings but complicit in the same game. It is through this ambiguous conjunction of a subjective series (authenticity) and an objective series (code, social consensus, commercial value), through this inflected sign, that the system of consumption can operate (FCPES: 105).

In modern art the artist begins to copy himself (for example, in Rauschenberg's work), that is the artist enters into the prose of the 'gestural elaboration of creation – spots, lines, dribbles ... ' And so the logic 'which was representation ... becomes repetition' (FCPES: 106). It is typical that Baudrillard's analysis jumps from the prose of the world to identify the logic of the 'empty gesture' of the series (for example, in the work of Warhol). This art is no longer a bourgeois art form, it is a form of art which attempts to reconcile itself with its own image, and becomes highly collusive and even homogeneous with the world of modern commercial culture. The social and cultural order is not disturbed by this kind of art, for the work of art enters culture simply as one more fashion item (FCPES: 108).

In another chapter, Baudrillard, in analysing the modern system of objects, gives a fuller picture of the steps taken in practice towards the modern system. We have moved, he argues, from the system of commodities as described by Marx, where things are produced for markets and their exchange-values reflect their utility, to a system of objects. The object, he argues, is different from the commodity and only comes into existence with the specific project inaugurated by the Bauhaus school of design. This new development is strictly analogous to the first emergence of the commodity system, as there are parallel processes at work. The elements of the initial system are violently disengaged so that the milieu becomes a functioning system of new aesthetic values and a battlefield for the 'mastery of signs' (FCPES: 187). The revolution in production, the industrial revolution (and the counter-discourses of romanticism and subjective poetry), is followed, according to Baudrillard, with another, a semiotic revolution of representation, in which 'sign-exchange' and fashion cycles become an operational semiology of a consumer society (FCPES: 187). Craft art practices which were previously distinct and separate from one another now become organised and synchronised into a system with its own code and syntax, and these function 'according to the same model' (FCPES: 190). This development is driven by a demand for functionality (yet it is a functionality which immediately finds itself in crisis, since it inevitably produces, from the standpoint of the human subject, strange and irrational counter-discourses). The Bauhaus aestheticisation of functional design, where the object is taken beyond the commodity, is accompanied by surrealist art, which plays on and mocks function, and by kitsch, which vulgarises it. Surrealism plays on and closes the gap between the aestheticised object and its 'abstract' purpose (FCPES: 193). It splits or fuses sign and function. It therefore never attempts to restore the symbolic relation which here is 'distorted and made into a phantasm' (FCPES: 193). Kitsch vulgarises by playing on the status of pseudo-object, through the 'superabundance of signs, of allegorical references, disparate connotations ... saturation by details' (CS: 110).

If surrealism is the effective counter-discourse of the first stage of the object (that is, the Bauhaus stage), abstractionism is the effective counter-discourse of the second stage of the object (the stage of 'cybernetic design') in which surrealism is relegated to the status of an outdated folkloric genre (FCPES: 194). And this second stage, of whatever form of abstraction, 'dreamlike, geometric or expressionist', from Klee to Pollock, is the last 'critical' stage of art (FCPES: 195). These observations on the stages of the evolution of art were complemented in this essay of 1972 with an attempt to build up a theory of the social changes which correlate with them. Baudrillard's key example of the kind of logic which becomes significant with sign-exchange is the art auction. In fact there is in Baudrillard's analysis virtually no discussion of any auctioning, or of art museums which are said to be the banks of (feudal) sumptuary value (FCPES: 122). In order to understand contemporary forms of social stratification and domination, it is essential, he argues, to grasp the fact that the formal process of exploitation (through market exchange) under capitalism is at this stage complemented by a re-emergence of sumptuary value and with it the assertion of aristocratic prestige. Baudrillard adopts here the anthropological problematic of Georges Bataille (FCPES: 117) where the object is theorised outside equivalence, as unique, as an aristocratic 'parity'. This is privilege realised outside of bourgeois exchange, and it induces an 'object-fetishism' as a mode of expenditure alongside commodity exchange. This form, developed within the capitalist frame at the stage of the emergence of the object system, becomes the 'keystone of domination' in bourgeois society and the principal form of class reproduction in the system. Thus only a thoroughly reconstructed Marxism can grasp that

> at the very heart of the economic mode of domination [capital] reinvents ... the logic and the strategy of signs, of castes, of segregation, and of discrimination; how it reinstates the feudal logic of personal relations or even that of gift exchange ... of agonistic exchange – in order simultaneously to thwart and crown the 'modern' socio economic logic of class. (FCPES: 120)

It is at this point that Baudrillard introduces one of his first analyses of simulacra. The forms of aristocratic expenditure and consumption are reproduced institutionally and become models:

> Only the mass-mediated simulacra of competition operate ... the great dinosaurs of 'wasteful expenditure' are changed into innumerable individuals pledged to a parody of sacrificial consumption, mobilized as consumers by the order of production ... Even the simulation model of a differential aristocratic code still acts as a powerful model of integration and control ... Everywhere prestige haunts our industrial societies, whose bourgeois culture is never more than the phantom of aristocratic values. (FCPES: 119)

This idea seems to be born from within the Marxist problematic; indeed, Baudrillard suggests that it is only by developing the framework in this way that theory can 'recapture Marx's analysis on a global level' (FCPES: 122). This thesis therefore has to be understood in its radical sense: modern consumers continue feudal relations under the impress of the simulacral discipline of bourgeois market relations on the one hand, and the simulation model of aristocratic expenditure both reproduces class discrimination and legitimates the system on the other.

After this critical moment, art itself in its traditional sense becomes impossible, since the 'hyper-reality of systems has absorbed the critical surreality of the phantom' into its own 'metadesign' (FCPES: 195). What is left of art is only 'lumino-dynamic manipulation or ... the psychedelic staging of a flaccid surrealism'; all else falls under the aegis of the hyperreal programme and the fashion cycle. Art and anti-art enter into and play the same game, and obey the 'same economy of the sign' (FCPES: 195–8).

Transaesthetic forms

There is in Baudrillard's work *Symbolic Exchange and Death* (1976), an analysis of baroque forms. Here the culture of the baroque is characterised by the appearance of a project to create an 'earthly demiurgy, the transubstantiation of all nature into a single substance ... Stucco is the triumphant democracy of all artificial signs' (SED: 51). Here, says Baudrillard, there is an attempt to create a unified substance which will enable 'phenomena to be ordered and separated at will'. Here the counterfeit 'still only works on substance and form, not yet on relations and structures, but at this level it is already aiming at control' (SED: 53). This is significant since it is clear that Baudrillard does at one level think in terms of an expansion of modes and spheres of domination. This is the germ of the idea of the emergence of transpolitical forms: in the baroque period the impetus of the transpolitical invades partial elements (transubstantiation) and only through subsequent decisive shifts becomes more comprehensive, through even the phase of fascism (where there is a transpoliticisation of a people by race and blood (DG: 118), embracing finally the transaesthetic itself:

> Art has ... failed to realize the utopian aesthetic of modern times, to transcend itself and become an ideal form of life. (In earlier times, of course, art had no need of self-transcendence, no need to become a totality, for such a totality already existed ...). Instead of being subsumed in a transcendent ideality, art has been dissolved within a general aestheticization of everyday life, giving way to a pure circulation of images, a transaestheticization of banality. Indeed, art took this route even before capital, for if the decisive

political event was the strategic crisis of 1929, whereby capital debouched into the era of mass transpolitics, the crucial moment for art was undoubtedly that of Dada and Duchamp, that moment when art, by renouncing its own aesthetic rules of the game, debouched into the transaesthetic era of the banality of the image. (TE: 11)

This thesis is confidently handled as the irruption of new forms into an already established tradition.

It is striking, then, that Baudrillard has a very sure idea of what he means by culture: it 'is a site of the secret, of initiation, of a restrained and highly ritualized symbolic exchange' (SS: 64), not to be confused with 'culture with a big C, the ideology of culture'(BL: 23), as is typically encountered in Europe (for in California 'I find myself freed from all culture' (BL: 131)). This view of culture as the site of initiation is consistently opposed as a form of exchange with the semiotic and simulation (EC). A recent discussion of the symbolic and semiotic suggests: 'they each follow their own course ... occasionally their collision or subduction creates fault lines into which reality rushes' (PC: 97). There are orders of simulacra and in each there appear, in the Baudrillard account, critical or ironic responses. Thus Warhol is important for Baudrillard because his work registers the originality of the 'irruption of simulation' (BL: 25). This response can, he says, be compared with that of Baudelaire to the commodity: Baudelaire does not analyse the commodity as a form of alienation or as fetishism of that form. Nor does Baudelaire anticipate Benjamin's analysis of the loss of aura as the inauguration of a melancholy modern culture. Baudrillard suggests that Baudelaire's response is the superior one since it immediately explores the new forms of seduction of 'pure objects and events' and its equivalent 'modern passion' identified as 'fascination' (FS: 118–19). Thus Baudelaire relates to the irruption of commodities in a new way: this 'is no longer a matter of the mastery of conventional effects, the mastery of illusion and of the aesthetic order, but rather of the vertigo of obscenity'. Thus, for Baudelaire, the work of art can be read as a 'new and triumphant fetish ... [which] should work to deconstruct its own traditional aura, its authority and power of illusion, in order to shine resplendent in the pure obscenity of the commodity' (FS: 118). It is therefore in relation to Baudelaire's concept of the absolute commodity, taking inspiration from the Universal Exhibition of 1855, that Baudrillard himself is inspired to an invocation of the object which 'must annihilate itself as a familiar object and become monstrously foreign ... [and which] glows with a veritable seduction that comes from elsewhere, from having exceeded its own form and become pure object, pure event' (FS: 118). It was not Benjamin, says Baudrillard, but Baudelaire who had 'the only real response, esthetic and metaphysical, ironical and joyous, to the challenge'

(FS: 119). It is not a question of a passive acceptance, or a melancholy critical reading, of the irruption of new forms. The pivotal question is to find the right affirmative response to them.

   Clearly for Baudrillard it is the wrong response which predominates today. For him the current situation is that

> art is currently reappropriating the works of the – distant, recent or even contemporary – past ... Now, admittedly, this reappropriation is supposed to be ironic. But the humour here is merely the transparent invocation of humour. Like the worn threads of a piece of fabric, it is an irony produced only by the disillusion of things, a fossilized irony. The little trick of placing the nude from Manet's *Déjeuner sur l'Herbe* opposite Cézanne's *Card Players*, as one might put an admiral's hat on a monkey, is nothing more than the advertising style irony currently engulfing the world of art. It is the irony of repentence and *ressentiment* towards one's own culture ... characteristic of radical disillusionment. It is as though history were rifling through its own dustbins and looking for redemption in the rubbish. (IE: 25–6)

This for Baudrillard is the last, the 'ultimate stage' in the history of art.

Photography

In an interview in 1991 replying to a question from Monique Arnaud, Baudrillard said: 'I have only been doing photography for four or five years. I am fascinated by it, it's something very intense. It's the form of the object, the form of the appearance of the object ... I like photography … as something that preserves the idea of a silent apparition' (BL: 23). But from his earliest writings in the 1960s Baudrillard has written on the photograph. In *For a Critique of the Political Economy of the Sign,* however, he was careful not to overestimate the importance of the invention of photography; he noted that modifications in painting practices could not be explained by the emergence of the photograph (FCPES: 81). The first important association with photography in his mature writing is the essay called *Please Follow Me*, intended as a theoretical commentary on Sophie Calle's exhibition: *Suite Vénitienne* (1983). Many versions of Baudrillard's essay have appeared, for example in *Fatal Strategies* (FS: 129ff.) and *The Transparency of Evil* (TE: 162ff.). In this essay the main theme is that of shadowing and seduction (which is opposed to Christian love (FS: 104–5)), as Baudrillard reflects on how S. follows a man and photographs the trajectory of his visit to Venice. Baudrillard writes in *Please Follow Me*: 'The shadowing makes the other vanish ... and photography is itself an art of disappearance ... ' (PFM: 86). In *Fatal Strategies* he writes: 'These are not the snapshot memories of a presence, but shots of an absence – that of the person followed, of the follower, and even of their absence from one another' (FS: 131).

But by the time of the next essay on Sophie Calle in *The Transparency of Evil*, many of the main elements have been reversed. The central problem of art now is described as 'entering into him as his shadow, as his double ... by embracing the Other the better to wipe out his tracks' (TE: 159). Photography is here situated in a different thematic, that of reconstituting the 'secret form of the other ... as in anamorphosis, starting with the fragments and tracing its broken lines, its lines of fracture' (TE: 155). Photography can attain the purest of images if it strips away subjectivity and becomes the 'conduit of pure objectality, permeable to a subtler kind of seduction' (TE: 154). Gradually, then, Baudrillard's ideas change. Instead of emphasising disappearance, he suggests photography is the mode par excellence of the 'pure image' (TE: 154). In *The Perfect Crime* he suggests that the effect of the photograph is to allow privileged access to a presence: 'Whatever the violence, speed or noise which surrounds it, it gives the object back its immobility and its silence. In the greatest of turbulence, it recreates the equivalence of the desert, of the stillness of phenomena' (PC: 86).

So gone is the thesis that photography concerns the 'vanished presence' of the other (PFM: 86): this has been replaced by that of the other's 'secret alterity ... we should look for the mask beneath identity ... ' But we should even look for 'the figure which haunts us and diverts us from our identities – the masked divinity which, in effect, haunts each of us for a moment, one day or another' (PC: 88). In a striking move, Baudrillard suggests that photography 'involves restoring to the world the formal power of illusion, which is precisely the same as becoming again, in an immanent way, a "thing among things"' (PC: 88). And by 1999 the photograph is nothing short of being a 'miracle, [for] this so called "objective" image, is that because the world reveals itself as radically non-objective' (EI: 175). Between the camera and the world there is a complicity between the 'objectivity' of the camera and the 'objectivity' of the object. Thus photography is not an art of mastery of the object, but enters into a game of finding 'a literality of the object, against meaning and the aesthetic of meaning ... ' When there is such an apparition the 'magical ... disappearance of reality' is achieved (EI: 176–7). If Baudrillard reintroduces the phenomenological frame, it is a 'wild' phenomenology (EI: 178); here the key argument is that the camera, or rather 'the photographic gaze, does not sound out or make an analysis of "reality" it rests "literally" on the surface of things' and for a brief moment illustrates (*illustre*) their fragmentary apparitions (EI: 177).

We can see then that in the early eighties Baudrillard was mainly concerned with seduction and the disappearance of the subject through the object, and this informs his commentary on photography. In the eighties he became a photographer himself. Some of his own photos were included in Marite Bonnal's *Passages* (Bonnal 1986); indeed, one of them (Ibid. 12) was later reproduced in Baudrillard's own collection of photos (Baudrillard 1998c: no. 67). The first essay specifically devoted to the theory of photography was published in *The Transparency of Evil* (TE: 156–61). Subsequently photography is discussed in *The Perfect Crime* (PC: 85–9), *Paroxysm* (P: 89–101) and in essays in Zurbrugg's *Jean Baudrillard: Art and Artefact* (Zurbrugg 1997: 32–42), as well as in *L'Échange impossible* (EI: 175–84).

How can this evolution of Baudrillard's thought be accounted for? Can this specific evolution be indicative of his own key theoretical trajectory? Certainly this seems possible. Reading Baudrillard's essays since his book *Seduction* reveals a sustained but not entirely consistent attempt to think through the shift into indeterminacy. In *Fatal Strategies* he tried to theorise this in terms of a development within modern science: the move towards chance, probability, and so on, is described as remaining within modern science, albeit as a form of hyper-rationality. Baudrillard called this the 'first' revolution (FS: 163). But more significant is the second revolution, which Baudrillard described as not only the aleatory 'floating of all laws' (FS: 163) in uncertainty, but as going beyond this to a situation where reversibility becomes a characteristic form of laws: that is not just the reversibility of 'particles into anti-particles, matter into anti-matter, but the laws themselves' (FS: 163). It is not certainty or uncertainty which is crucial, but, in the last analysis, reversibility.

By the end of the 1980s Baudrillard has stepped back to argue that the crucial revolution is that of uncertainty, has developed his notions of transfinite or transpolitical forms, and has defined the nature of the transition from third- to fourth-order simulacra, described as going beyond alienation, 'in the same direction' (TE: 173), following the object as strange attractor. 'All that remains' after the end of the dialectic and alienation 'is a lack of determinancy as to the position of the subject and the position of the other' (TE: 122). The subject falls into self-propagation. In biology the end of the dialectic brings the regime of replication, cloning; in art it brings the series and simulation. In this new situation where there is no dialectic of positive and negative, both terms and all aesthetic oppositions begin to outbid themselves, so that once freed from reality, we move to the more real than real – hyperrealism. 'It was in fact with hyperrealism and pop art that everything began, that everything was raised to the ironic power of photographic realism' (TE: 18). Here Baudrillard notes a place for photography in an alignment with hyperrealism.

There is hyperrealism as an intensification of the real. But there is also the transaesthetic of the real where all the forms become indifferent to themselves, having gone beyond their own power, and where 'nothing in this sphere conflicts with anything else. Neo-Geometricism, Neo-Expressionism, New Abstraction, New Representationalism – all co-exist with a marvellous facility amid general indifference' (TE: 15). It is as if the art which 'had developed magnificently over several centuries had suddenly been immobilized' (TE: 15). It is a stage which might be described as that equivalent to the floating of laws, the impact of loss of determinant boundaries. Here it is only the negative charge which has intensity: Warhol's Campbell's soup can 'releases us from the need to decide between the beautiful and the ugly, between the real and the unreal, between transcendence and immanence' (TE: 17).

But in *The Perfect Crime*, Baudrillard suggests that Warhol can be seen as the first artist 'to have reached the stage of radical fetishism, the stage beyond alienation – the paradoxical stage of an otherness raised to perfection. This is what earned him ... that fetishistic aura which attaches to the singularity of the void' (PC: 79). Warhol presents an artist as mutant, as an extreme phenomenon, as paradox. Thus there is intensity, but it is paradoxically achieved: ' ... it is by preserving this indifference of images to the world and our own (Warholian) indifference to images that we preserve their virulence and their intensity' (PC: 81). And, importantly, Warhol does not attempt to represent reality, or indeed the world. This returns art in a certain way to the prose of the world; but in the case of Warhol, he 'does not represent it: he is a fragment of it: a fragment in the pure state' (PC: 84). We should not forget, however, that Warhol's fragments, like Baudrillard's photographs in publications and exhibitions, have signatures.

CHAPTER 10

Conclusion

> It's possible that ... there's also a millenarian
> dimension to all this! I'd have no objection to that.
> You don't escape your own culture. (P: 45)

Whether we consider Derrida, Virilio, Althusser, or Comte, Marx, Nietzsche or Baudrillard, all remain within the framework of messianic time, its acceleration or deceleration, its elation or deflation. What seems to happen is a repeated pattern of extreme expectation and promise followed by postponement and waiting, but all within a common frame. Norman Cohn's work has traced this pattern in Western culture from the Zoroastrians.[1] The pattern is repeated with the early Christians and of course with the political utopians in the 1840s, and again in the 1960s. All the current variations seem on the face of it to be little more than intellectual manoeuvres, a 'playing with vestiges', pure *bricolage*. But this is a serious misreading, at times fostered by these authors themselves.

Messianic variations

In the mid nineteenth century, and again in the 1960s, intellectuals, particularly leading French ones, believed they stood on the threshold of a new age. Theory was conceived and experienced under the tension of an impending, inevitable and terrible but ineluctable event. Theory now is conceived either under the threat of an event which must not take place, which must at all costs be deferred (Derrida and Virilio) or under the sign of a fatal event which has already happened. But what if the initiative has passed (for the moment) to the object, as if the world has passed a threshold and reached a new condition? This can be thought of as a quite new disjunction between action and judgement. Thus unlike the resolution proposed by Comte and perhaps also by Althusser, where the lived world is refigured by intellectuals as scientific fetishism or ideology, the solution proposed by Baudrillard is that such a fetishism, now infused with an unprecedented technological seduction, has slipped out of the distracted control of the subject. As for the messiah, 'He will not come on the day of the Last Judgement, but on the day after.'[2]

Here it is instructive to compare and contrast a number of messianic variations amongst leading French theorists: for example, the strange vision described by Caputo where deconstruction 'is an operation that keeps the future structurally open and structurally unknown ...Were we to come upon the Messiah, dressed in rags, we would still have to ask, "when will you come?" Derrida wants to defer and delay the parousia, to hold it off. (Don't come!)'(Caputo 1997: 245); this vision effectively reverses the structure of desire in traditional forms of messianism, as Derrida himself is at pains to emphasise. According to Derrida, the West

> has been dominated by a powerful program that was also an untransgressible contract among discourses of the end ...To be sure there are obvious differences between Hegelian eschatology, that Marxist eschatology people have too quickly wanted to forget ... Nietzschean eschatology (between the last man, the higher man, and the overman), and so many other more recent varieties. But aren't these differences measured as deviations in relation to a fundamental tonality of this *Stimmung* audible across so many thematic variations?'[3]

It might be expected that Derrida begin a deconstruction of this grid and reveal it as the frame of the Western metaphysical system; at least this is what many readers of his earlier writings have led us to expect. But Derrida has a surprise for his interpreters: deconstruction does not attempt to step outside this frame. His essay called 'On an Apocalyptic Tone Newly Adopted in Philosophy', does not follow Kant's line in his 1796 essay 'On a Newly Raised Superior Tone in Philosophy', which lampoons pretentious mystagogy as a threat to philosophy itself. Despite the observations of Christopher Norris,[4] it is clear that Derrida adopts the apocalyptic tone himself. Derrida explains: 'I wanted ... to mime in citation but also transform into a genre, and then parody, deport, deform the well-known title.'

One can easily imagine the immediate reaction of progressive rationalists to this move, just as one has already encountered the reactions of Emile Littre and John Stuart Mill to the religious turn in Auguste Comte's writing in the 1840s: as a deplorable resurrection of superstition. But what is striking in both Comte and Derrida is that the move is made with intellectual conviction within a highly rationalist, even artificial, philosophical frame. It is a move which allows them not only to talk about the body and human emotions, but also to make 'surprising' discoveries about bodily functions. Comte's Catholic-rationalist formation allowed him to announce the thesis that the true function of human sexuality lies neither in reproduction nor sensual pleasure but in the moral benefits which can be derived through sublimation and chastity: human reproduction will occur in this utopia of the virgin either through 'material means, but especially by a better action of the nervous on the vascular system', that is, parthenogenesis (Comte 1854: 242). Derrida's Jewish-rationalist formation allows him to make discoveries about circumcision, but his most surprising discovery is that:

deep down, deep down inside, the eye would be destined not to see but to weep. For at the very moment they veil sight, tears would unveil what is proper to the eye ... to have imploration rather than vision in sight, to address prayer, love, joy, or sadness rather than a look or a gaze. Even before it illuminates, revelation is the moment of the 'tears of joy'.(Derrida 1990: 126)

The difference between Comte and Derrida is that Comte, in believing the time had come for the new religion, set himself up as the high priest of the religion of humanity and immediately laid down its sacraments (precisely the type of mystagogy Kant attacked). Derrida, on the other hand, offers only an appeal for a 'New International' arising on the implosion of the communist movement. Comte initiated the new ecclesiastical organisation because the events on the ground had not worked out in the way he had predicted: the famous law of the three states predicted the imminence of the third and final rationalist utopia. Comte's appeal to fetishism and 'sociocracy' was a postmodern invention (just as his invention of sociology was modernist), made necessary because historical evolution appeared to procrastinate, delaying, frustratingly, the final transition. Derrida is in a similar position since the attempts to realise the 'third state' as a paradise of one kind or another have all failed or disappointed. Derrida's thought had moved in this disenchanted messianic direction well before the collapse of the USSR, and he was suitably prepared to deal with 'Soviet Marxism'.

Althusser's position was quite different from that of Derrida. Althusser, once the Catholic militant, then in the 1960s the 'high priest' of Marxism, for example wrote 'the inevitable transitional phase of socialism which Marx spoke about is "a load of crap"'. This is a phrase he repeated, for in his later writings Althusser had become altogether disenchanted with the socialist road. The idea of a proletarian party trying to cross the 'vast river of shit' is really only an eschatological vision 'with which we are all utterly bored'. His evident resignation and disillusionment is clear: 'I am not sure whether humanity will ever experience communism, that eschatological view of Marx' (Althusser 1992: 224–6, translation modified (MG)). But instead of suggesting that the revolution will simply explode when no one expects it, he argued that 'oases of communism already exist' in the interstices of market and class relations, just as merchant capital existed within feudalism. The function of the intellectual is to aid the existing and potential mass movements which produce these oases, to learn from their action and to avoid repeating mistakes. The obvious problem here for a Marxist like Althusser is that in saying that these oases exist outside structures of exploitation, he still leaves the problem of how the dominant structures of exploitation are to be overthrown. The way seemed open here for Althusser to move towards Benjamin's historical materialism which 'cannot do without the notion of a present which is not a transition, but in which time stands still and has come to a stop ... the sign of a Messianic cessation' (Benjamin 1970: 264–5). But Althusser's theoretical turn against the strategy of the 'transitional state' opens the door to the messianic irruption only to shut it firmly again in a rejection of all eschatology. It also leaves the conception dangerously dependent on the one remaining purity, the uncorrupted support: the masses, the people who perform the double function of actor and judge at the right moment, the appropriate but increasingly unpredictable encounter (Elliott 1998).

It is here that the particularity of Derrida's position on Marxism becomes clear. Like Althusser, Derrida was intently suspicious of all the organisations formed under the banner of revolutionary Marxism. But for Derrida unlike Comte or Marx or Althusser, it is the very structure of the messianic which is revolutionary: it 'would be urgency, imminence but, irreducible paradox, a waiting without horizon of expectation' (Derrida 1993: 168). Thus in a sense we must not know what is to come if there is to be hope and justice. If we do know and there is simply a programmed road, there may be law but no justice. Here we find a certain *rapprochement* with the work of Virilio on the technological threat to the messianic. Derrida raises the very

> possibility of virtual events whose movement and speed prohibit us more than ever ... from opposing presence to its representation, 'real time' to 'deferred time', effectivity to its simulacrum, the living to the non-living, in short the living to the living-dead of its ghosts. It [the differential employment of tele-technology] obliges us to think, from there another space for democracy. (Ibid. 168)

So even democracy is threatened in the way Virilio has suggested by the impact of a technology bent on speeding up and simulating the event. Indeed, for Derrida 'the messianic trembles on the edge of this event itself' (Ibid. 169). The question is thus transformed, for instead of dreaming the utopia and programming its realisation, the problem becomes 'how to give rise and to give place, still, still to render it habitable, but without killing the future in the name of old frontiers?' (Ibid.). Thus the problem is to distinguish between eschatology and teleology, and to hold off the political and technological closures threatening the habitable, democratic spaces. Like Virilio, Derrida here appears to say the world is going too fast. Virilio indeed has called for a grey ecology: a movement against the pollution of speed (Virilio 1997: 58–68). Slow down or democratic time will be lost. Grey procrastination.

This is where Derrida and Virilio, on the one side, and Baudrillard, on the other, fall out. Baudrillard's writing in the 1970s was influenced decisively by millenarianism, but in quite a different way from that of Derrida. In his vigorous and explicitly messianic critique of scientific Marxism of 1973 he contrasts the Marx of the 1840s with the Marx of the 1860s: there is a transition, a 'conversion from the here and now to an asymptotic fulfilment' (MP: 161). Utopianism is 'never written for the future'. In *Symbolic Exchange and Death* (SED: 186) Baudrillard conceived that the way in which Benjamin's vision (Benjamin 1970: 244) of a humanity experiencing 'its own destruction as an aesthetic pleasure' could be read as a version of the last judgement, 'there already, realised: the definitive spectacle of our crystallised death', as if the world was realising itself as a terrifying utopia 'here and now'. In his famous critique of Foucault, *Forget Foucault*, Baudrillard turned this into a messianic parable uniting Nietzsche and Kafka as alternative sources: Baudrillard's neo-Nietzschean formulation suggests that 'the Messiah of the day after is only a God resuscitated from among the dead' (FF: 60). Nietzsche's own explanation of the death of God is often taken to be the highly unlikely idea that 'he died of pity for man' but even here the actual enunciation is more complex: it is Zarathustra who says, 'Thus spoke the Devil to me once: "Even God has his Hell: it is his love for man." And I lately heard him say these words: "God is dead; God has died of his pity for man"' (Nietzsche 1969: 114).

Baudrillard gives this parable a surprising reading. First he asks, is it therefore perhaps not the case that in effect 'things have never needed the Messiah or the Revolution to take place?' This is an obvious, important questioning of the mystagogy of religious and political events as decisive causal connections themselves – a question few theorists ask. But secondly, 'the Revolution signifies only this: that it has already taken place' (FF: 50), a theme developed at great length in Baudrillard's subsequent writings. The rendezvous, at the right moment, of revolutionary theory and the Revolution, of the messiah with the Last Judgement, did not take place. Yet something occured and is repeated as an essentially misaligned encounter, always out of joint, dislocated. This version, like Derrida's, saves the problematic of messianic time, it does not get outside it. It does not, however, have to depend on weak and improbable teleological optimism, which still rests on the synchrony of the messianic coming and the right moment of judgement. (Derrida's pleading prayer to the messiah – 'don't come: procrastinate, for if You come the world will become uninhabitable' – implies this synchrony.) Baudrillard has no need of prayers, for the world let go of the frame, 'the catastrophe is behind us':

> This reversing of the sign of catastrophe is the exceptional privilege of our age. It liberates us from any future catastrophe and any responsibility in that regard. The end of all anticipatory psychoses, all panic, all remorse! The lost object is behind us. We are free of the Last Judgement. (IE: 121)

But the messianic does not disappear, Baudrillard locates it not as a uniquely Western form, but as the universal structure of all symbolic forms; the event without precedent is seduction; it is also without origin, coming from somewhere else and arriving always unexpectedly – a pure event that erases in one fell swoop all conscious and unconscious determination. And because it is without precedent it 'liberates us' from genesis and history. (FS: 138)

Radical theory

Yet in an important sense Baudrillard no longer, if he ever did, reads utopian analysis as implying the need to construct imaginary ideal worlds – the temptation to idealise either primitive cultures and their symbolic systems, or future communist egalitarian societies. So the argument of this book about Baudrillard can be summed up by saying that in the 1990s his work has indeed taken on a new shape, and this in itself demands a rethinking of all his earlier writings. At the beginning of the book, it was argued that Baudrillard's own idea of the double spiral (of symbol around sign) was the clearest and best way of grasping the overall shape of his trajectory. At the end, it is clear that his work is not a single seamless argument, but can be seen to involve as well as the two basic 'paradigms' of the double spiral, the combination of what I shall call here two basic 'thematics' (technically there are more, but here they are condensed to two). The first is that of Marx (extended and developed through additions of Bataille (who also brings Mauss), Benjamin, Marcuse, Barthes, McLuhan, and many others, including Lacan); and Baudrillard also invokes scientific reason, which broadly gives the historical scope and frame of his analysis, including its emphasis on technology. The second is that of Nietzsche and Bataille again (but a Bataille who allows Baudrillard to fuse Nietzsche with Hölderlin, Baudelaire, Rimbaud, Jarry, the Situationists, and others such as Canetti and Gombrowicz).

If we read Baudrillard in this way, we identify a number of key elements in his work, its styles, its objectives, its transformations, within a relatively stable frame. First of all, it is clear that this frame involves a radical comparative anthropology. In the earliest writings, this identified the symbolic as ambivalent against the univocality of the sign. Then he updated Bataille and Mauss through an elaboration of the symbolic order as found in primitive cultures (outlining in 1976 a research programme which is still continuing). But very quickly the theory of the symbolic order was replaced by a theory of forms, particularly of seduction and fatal strategies. Two striking aspects of this anthropology were, first, its reading of the relation between symbolic, imaginary and the real, a reading influenced decisively by Saussure and Lacan; and secondly, its reading of the primitive double as quite different from the forms of the alienated double found, for example, in Christianity, a thesis taken from Nietzsche. This complex anthropological theory of forms has become a relatively stable base for Baudrillard's theory of the radical otherness of symbolic cultures, and in some crucial respects has taken on the status of a doctrine.

Baudrillard does not elaborate or 'fill in' the historical sequence of European development from antiquity to the Renaissance. But his (Nietzschean) critique of Marxism (*The Mirror of Production*) allows us to reconstruct it in outline. His work is essentially focused in an analysis of Western cultures since the Renaissance which fuses the two thematics (Marx, Nietzsche) in an original way. One key aspect of this writing is the importance it gives to the present (and future): if the current conjuncture changes, a new logic becomes predominant and this changes everything. Knowledge, problematics, practices, rapidly become obsolete. Theory has to anticipate obsolescence and, as he notes, pays a high price. Thus if his ideas appear nostalgic and sometimes reactionary, they attempt at the same time to be at the edge of new developments in science and technology, developments which are simultaneously creative and, necessarily, highly destructive. Thus if we look at Marxist theory from Baudrillard's perspective, the orders of simulacral forms map on to pre-industrial (sixteenth to eighteenth century) capitalism, industrial capitalism, monopoly capitalism, and what might be called post-monopoly 'capitalism' (in the last third of the twentieth century). It was with the emergence of monopoly capitalism that the 'mode of production' model gave way to determination by the code (*The Mirror of Production*), so Baudrillard delimits the applicability of classical Marxism to a period which Marx himself saw passing away: Marx's theory was not radical enough. The subsequent emphasis of Marxists on proletarian revolution and the economic simply played into the hands of the system, which now works on a higher logic.

But Baudrillard retains all the trappings of historico-conjunctural analysis elaborated by Marxists, particularly French Marxists in the 1960s. Almost all of Baudrillard's essays analyse socio-cultural shifts, or rely on such comparisons, with the understanding that the world has far outstripped earlier Marxist visions in the extreme radicality of forms. In Baudrillard's thematic developing Marx's ideas, theory not only moves beyond a reliance on the mode of production, but also now beyond the monopoly code, with its corresponding 'information revolution' within consumer society.

But this study has been concerned with another revolution identified by Baudrillard and which has occupied his thinking since the mid 1980s. It is possible to look for historical and conjunctural markers of such a shift. They would be the collapse of communism, the failure of the socialist project more generally, the shift to mass societies, emergence of post-colonialist global 'postmodern' culture, the attempt to develop a new world order, and so forth. For Baudrillard these are all highly significant, and he has written about them all. But there is another key element, that of the revolution in the sciences, and the shift into fundamental uncertainty at all levels in contemporary culture. Here Baudrillard's emphasis has to move to some extent from the *fatal* to what he has defined as radical theory. Taking the transition from ordered to chaotic universe in its strongest sense he has in the current situation identified as the crucial marker the uncertainty revolution that opened up in the sciences. This move takes Baudrillard back into the venerable tradition of the dialectics of nature (from Engels to Althusser), but in a new conjuncture. Radical theory in the natural sciences is raided for a new terminology to account for shifts in culture and society. Thus the whole apparatus of structural Marxism, with its adoption of the concepts of dialectical logic, alienation, contradiction and over-determination, is reconfigured using notions of exponential logic, transparency, chaos and hyperspace.

But why is Baudrillard fundamentally in opposition to contemporary Western cultural forms, and why does he think he can resort to the extreme ideas of hyper-modern science? The answer here lies with his adoption of the second thematic, derived fundamentally from Nietzsche's critique of Christian cultures. If Marx provides a telling account of the mechanisms of industrial capitalism, the formation of critical theory elaborates an alienated, 'unhappy' consciousness, quite parallel to that of Christian alienation. In their various forms of *ressentiment*, Christian and Marxist theories merge into a self-destructive nihilistic cultural matrix which also annihilates every other culture it encounters. Baudrillard opts for the life-affirming response of Nietzsche and Baudelaire against Marx and Benjamin. And in this study I have attempted to indicate the sort of judgements he has been trying to establish on the basis of this thematic: from Baudelaire to Warhol, into his own practices of writing and photography. It seems that Baudrillard has in each conjuncture tried to work out the right response to the critical cultural and political problems. It is certainly not a position which suggests, despite his insistence on the *fatal*, that there are no options. As was pointed out in the discussion of *The Dice Man* in the Preface, Baudrillard even attempts to demarcate the right response to the concept of uncertainty itself. Thus it might be said that he tries to rid the Marxist tradition, and critical theory, of all forms of *ressentiment* through a thoroughgoing Nietzschean critique, and to rid Nietzscheanism of its transhistorical elitism through a reconfigured Marxist critique. He is probably not the first to attempt this: such diverse writers as Max Weber and Georges Bataille have also done so, and even Althusser had something of this project in mind during his last period. Baudrillard's version arrives at radical theory in a unique way:

> Radical thought situates itself in the zone of impossible exchange, of non-equivalence, of the unintelligible, the undecidable. (P: 35)

Notes

Chapter 1

1. Steve Beard and Jim McClellan, 'Baudrillard', *The Face*, January 1989, pp. 61–2.
2. Peter Hamilton, 'One-man Think Tank', *Sunday Times*, 11 December 1994.
3. Chris Horrocks, 'Death on the Net', *Icon Review*, Autumn 1996, p. 8.
4. Michael Fordham, 'Jean Baudrillard', *Dazed and Confused*, 31 (1997), p. 80.
5. William Leith, 'Jean Baudrillard', *Observer* (Life), 15 February 1998, pp. 12–17.
6. Richard Gott, 'Standfirst', *Guardian*, 13 December 1994.
7. (FCM: 127). Richard Gott resigned as literary editor from the *Guardian* in December 1994 after revelations about his activities as a Soviet agent from Oleg Gordievsky, former KGB controller in London.
8. Asked about this, Baudrillard said his response to the paper at the conference was silence. As to the portrait: it was, he said, his double (*sosie*).
9. An article by Baudrillard conveyed for publication in the early 1990s was indeed a scissors and paste compilation with handwritten additions and deletions.
10. Genosko discusses at length what can be learnt from Baudrillard's interviews (Genosko 1998: 13–22).
11. See note 3.

Chapter 2

1. Baudrillard insists that this has nothing to do with being depressed, or of being a depressive (BL: 180).

Chapter 4

1. In Rex Butler's recent study, Baudrillard 'repeats the same essential paradox throughout his work', so in Butler's own book 'there can finally be no sequence to it or logic to the separation of its chapters'

(Butler 1999: 141). Baudrillard is concerned throughout with 'a real that is the limit to all systems, a real that no system could ever entirely capture or explain' and this 'real upon which the system cannot reflect ... is only the sign itself' (Ibid. 137). Butler is 'reading against' Baudrillard's concept. He admits at the end of the book that his purpose has been to 'produce an unrecognizable Baudrillard' (Ibid. 171), a metaphysics of semiosis strangely closer to that which Baudrillard once identified as the game of hide-and-seek with the real to be found in the thought of Lacan.

2. This opens Baudrillard up to a specific kind of objection: following Nietzsche, he has not appreciated the bifurcation in world religions exposed in Max Weber's celebrated critique of Nietzsche. Primitive religions, Eastern religions, are not all of the same type. Cargo cults and millenarian forms come into existence when they come into contact with Christian and Western monotheistic religions in conditions of extreme social tension. These religions themselves are found in two quite different time modalities: that of imminence, and that of deferment. Eastern religions themselves can also take on messianic forms and cannot be reduced to one type of orientation (to a way, or to polytheism). It seems that Baudrillard is not interested in working on a study of these forms and variations but is content to draw on them to reveal contrasts with Western forms.

Chapter 7

1. See the recent discussion of the limits of Derrida's contribution to feminism in Feder et al. 1997. John D. Caputo in this collection concludes:

> The deep strand in Derrida's work ... the thought that does not contradict but reorientates his Nietzschean side, is the 'thought' of the 'beyond', of justice as the 'impossible' something that will create an alternative and free us all from the straits of identity. Derrida's feminism, then, takes the form of the delimitation of gender ... The two genders, masculine and feminine, not one more, not one less, to which each of us, one by one, is implacably destined ... Do they not dominate and manipulate us all, narrow us and confine us, making us all less than we can be, blocking off the 'beyond' and an absolute future to come? ... Maybe we are to be visited by the most amazing transformations of gender, in the blink of an eye ... (Ibid. 157)

Chapter 8

1. Michael Fordham, 'Jean Baudrillard', *Dazed and Confused*, 31 (1997), p. 80.

Chapter 10

1. Cohn 1993; see also Cohn's chapter 'How Time Acquired a Consummation', in Bull 1995: 21–37.
2. Kafka, cited in FF: 49.
3. Jacques Derrida, 'On an Apocalyptic Tone Newly Adopted in Philosophy', in Coward & Foshay 1992: 48.
4. Christopher Norris, 'Versions of the Apocalypse: Kant, Derrida, Foucault', in Bull 1995: 236. The very curious note to Norris's essay is interesting from the point of view of procrastination. It says that Norris's lecture notes on this topic 'proved too long (and too detailed in certain aspects of its argument) for inclusion ... he therefore decided to substitute the present article' (Ibid. 247).

Bibliography

Anderla, G., Dunning, A. and Forge S. (1997): *Chaotics: An Agenda for Business and Society in the 21ˢᵗ Century*. London: Adamantine Press.

Baudrillard, J. (1975): *The Mirror of Production*. St Louis: Telos.

Baudrillard, J. (1978): *L'Ange de stuc*. Paris: Galilee.

Baudrillard, J. (1981): *For a Critique of the Political Economy of the Sign*. St Louis: Telos.

Baudrillard, J. (1983): *In the Shadow of the Silent Majorities*. New York: Semiotext(e).

Baudrillard, J. (1985): *La Gauche divine*. Paris: Grasset.

Baudrillard, J. (1987): *Forget Foucault*. New York: Semiotext(e).

Baudrillard, J. (1988a): *America*. London: Verso.

Baudrillard, J. (1988b): *The Ecstasy of Communication*. New York: Semiotext(e).

Baudrillard, J. (1988c): *Please Follow Me*, with S. Calle, *Suite vénitienne*. Seattle: Bay Press.

Baudrillard, J. (1988d): *Jean Baudrillard: Selected Writings*, ed. M. Poster. Oxford: Polity.

Baudrillard, J. (1989): *Looking Back on the End of the World*. New York: Semiotext(e).

Baudrillard, J. (1990a): *Seduction*. London: Macmillan.

Baudrillard, J. (1990b): *Fatal Strategies*. London: Pluto.

Baudrillard, J. (1990c): *Cool Memories*. London: Verso.

Baudrillard, J. (1990d): *Revenge of the Crystal: Selected Writings*, London: Pluto.

Baudrillard, J. (1993a): *Baudrillard Live: Selected Interviews*. London: Routledge.

Baudrillard, J. (1993b): *Symbolic Exchange and Death*. London: Sage.

Baudrillard, J. (1993c): *The Transparency of Evil*. London: Verso.

Baudrillard, J. (1994a): *The Illusion of the End*. Cambridge: Polity.

Baudrillard, J. (1994b): *Simulacra and Simulation*. Ann Arbor: University of Michigan Press.

Baudrillard, J. (1995): *The Gulf War Did Not Take Place*. Sydney: Power.

Baudrillard, J. (1996a): *Cool Memories II*. Cambridge: Polity.

Baudrillard, J. (1996b): *The Perfect Crime*. London: Verso.

Baudrillard, J. (1996c): *The System of Objects*. London: Verso.

Baudrillard, J. (1997a): *Fragments. Cool Memories III*. London:Verso.

Baudrillard, J. (1997b): *Écran total*. Paris: Galilee.

Baudrillard, J. (1998a): *Paroxsym: Interviews with Phillipe Petit*. London: Verso.

Baudrillard, J. (1998b): *The Consumer Society: Myths and Structures*. London: Sage.

Baudrillard, J. (1998c): *Car l'illusion ne s'oppose pas a la realité*. Paris: Descartes.

Baudrillard, J. (1999a): *L'Échange impossible*. Paris: Galilee.

Baudrillard, J. (1999b): *Within the Horizon of the Object: Jean Baudrillard Photographs, 1995–1998*. Graz: Neue Galerie and Ostfildern-Ruit: Hatje Cantz.

Bauman, Z. (1992): *Intimations of Postmodernism*. London: Routledge.

Benjamin, W. (1970): *Illuminations*. London: Cape.

Best, S. (1989): 'The Commodification of Reality and the Reality of Commodification'. *Critical Perspectives in Social Theory*, 19: 3, 32–51.

Bogard, W. (1996): *The Simulation of Surveillance: Hypercontrol in Telematic Societies*. Cambridge: Cambridge University Press.

Bonnal, M. (1986): *Passages*. Paris: Galilee.

Borges, J.-L. (1970): *Labyrinths*. Harmondsworth: Penguin.

Bull, M. (ed.) (1995): *Apocalypse Theory and the Ends of the World*. Oxford: Blackwell.

Butler, R. (1999): *Jean Baudrillard: The Defence of the Real*. London: Sage.

Callinicos, A. (1989): *Against Postmodernism: A Marxist Critique*. Cambridge: Polity.

Caputo, J. (1997): *The Prayers and Tears of Jacques Derrida: Religion without Religion*. Bloomington: Indiana University Press.

Chapman, R. (ed.) (1988): *Male Order, Unwrapping Masculinity*. London: Lawrence and Wishart.

Coles, P. (ed.) (1998): *The New Cosmology*. Cambridge: Icon.

Cohn, N. (1993): *Cosmos, Chaos and the World to Come*. New Haven: Yale University Press.

Coward, H. and Foshay, T. (eds) (1992): *Derrida and Negative Philosophy*. New York: State University of New York Press.

Critchley, S. and Schroeder, W. (eds) (1998): *A Companion to Continental Philosophy*. Oxford: Blackwell.

Cushman, T. and Mestrovic, S. (eds) (1996): *This Time We Knew*. New York: New York University Press.

Denzin, N. (1991): *Images of Postmodern Society: Social Theory and Contemporary Cinema*. London: Sage.

Derrida, J. (1981): *Dissemination*. London: Athlone.

Derrida, J. (1990): *Memoirs of the Blind: The Self Portrait and Other Ruins*. Chicago: University of Chicago Press.

Derrida, J. (1993): *Spectres of Marx*. London: Routledge.

Doel, M. and Clarke, D. (1999): 'Virtual Worlds: Simulation, suppletion, s(ed)uction simulacra'. In Crang, M. and May, J. (eds): *Virtual Geographies, Bodies, Space and Relations*. London: Routledge.

Durkheim, E. (1982): *The Rules of Sociological Method*. London: Macmillan.

Elliott, G. (1998): 'Ghostlier Demarcations: On the Posthumous Edition of Althusser's Writings'. *Radical Philosophy*, 90, 20–32.

Feder, E., Rawlinson, M. and Zakin, E. (eds) (1977): *Derrida and Feminism*. London: Routledge.

Foucault, M. (1970): *The Order of Things*. London: Tavistock.

Foucault, M. (1977): *Discipline and Punish*. London: Allen Lane.

Frankovits, A. (ed.) (1984): *Seduced and Abandoned: The Baudrillard Scene*. Glebe: Stonemoss.

Gane, M. (1991a): *Baudrillard: Critical and Fatal Theory*. London: Routledge.

Gane, M. (1991b): *Baudrillard's Bestiary: Baudrillard and Culture*. London: Routledge.

Gane, M. (ed.) (2000): *Jean Baudrillard: Masters of Social Theory* (4 vols). London: Sage.

Genosko, G. (1992): 'The Struggle for Affirmative Weakness'. *Current Perspectives in Social Theory*, 12, 179–94.

Genosko, G. (1994): *Baudrillard and Signs: Signification Ablaze*. London: Routledge.

Genosko, G. (1998): *Undisciplined Theory*. London: Sage.

Genosko, G. (1999): *McLuhan and Baudrillard: The Masters of Implosion*. London: Routledge.

Gottdiener, M. (1995): *Postmodern Semiotics: Material Culture and the Forms of Modern Life*. Oxford: Blackwell.

Halperin, D. (1995): *Saint Foucault: A Gay Hagiography*. Oxford: Oxford University Press.

Horrocks, C. (1999): Baudrillard and the Millennium. Cambridge: Icon.

Jameson, F. (1991): *Postmodernism, or the Cultural Logic of Late Capitalism*. Durham N.C.: Duke University Press.

Kamper, D. and Wulf, C. (eds) (1989): *Looking Back at the End of the World*. New York: Semiotext(e).

Keeble, R. (1997): *Secret State, Silent Press: New Militarism, the Gulf and the Modern Image of Warfare*. Luton: University of Luton Press.

Kellner, D. (1989): *Jean Baudrillard: From Marxism to Postmodernity and Beyond*. Cambridge: Polity.

Kellner, D. (ed.) (1994): *Baudrillard: A Critical Reader*. Oxford: Blackwell.

Kroker, A. (1985): 'Baudrillard's Marx'. *Theory Culture and Society*, 2: 3, 69–83.

Kroker, A. (1992): *The Possessed Individual: Technology and Post-modernism*. London: Macmillan.

Kroker, A. and Cook, D. (eds) (1988): *The Postmodern Scene*. London: Macmillan.

Levin, C. (1996): *Jean Baudrillard: A Study of Cultural Metaphysics*. London: Prentice Hall.

Luke, T. W. (1991): 'Power and Politics in Hyperreality – The Critical Project of Jean Baudrillard'. *Social Science Journal*, 28: 3, 347–67.

Majastre, J.-O. (ed.) (1996): *Sans oublier Baudrillard*. Brussels: La Lettre Volée.

Merrin, W. (1994): 'Uncritical Criticism? Norris, Baudrillard and the Gulf War'. *Economy and Society*, 23: 2, 141–54.

Mestrovic, S. (1998): *Anthony Giddens, The Last Modernist*. London: Routledge.

Moore, S. (1988): 'Baudrillard – A Different Drummer. In Chapman, R. and Rutherford J. (eds), *Male Order: Unwrapping Masculinity*, London: Lawrence and Wishart.

Morris, M. (1988): *The Pirate's Fiancée*. London: Verso.

Moses, C. and Rabine, L. (eds) (1993): *Feminism, Socialism and French Romanticism*. Bloomington: Indiana University Press.

Nietzsche, F. (1969): *Thus Spoke Zarathustra*. Harmondsworth: Penguin.

Norris, C. (1989): 'Lost in the Funhouse: Baudrillard and the Politics of Postmodernism'. *Textual Practice*, 3: 3, 360–87.

Norris, C. (1992): *Uncritical Theory: Postmodernism and Society: Intellectuals and the Gulf War*. London: Lawrence and Wishart.

Parent, C. and Virilio, P. (1996): *The Function of the Oblique*. London: Architectural Association.

Poster, M. (1990) *The Mode of Information: Poststructuralism and Social Context*. Cambridge: Polity.

Poundstone, W. (1991): *Labyrinths of Reason*. Harmondsworth: Penguin.

Rhinehart, L. (1994): *The Dice Man*. London: HarperCollins.

Ritzer, G. (1997): *Postmodern Social Theory*. New York: McGraw-Hill.

Ritzer, G. (1999): *Enchanting a Disenchanted World: Revolutionizing the Means of Consumption*. London: Pine Forge.

Rojek, C. and Turner, B. (eds) (1993): *Forget Baudrillard?* London: Routledge.

Rotzer, G. (1995): *Conversations with French Philosophers*. New Jersey: Humanities Press.

Scruton, R. (1998): *An Intelligent Person's Guide to Modern Culture*. London: Duckworth.

Smart, B. (1990): 'On the Disorder of Things: Sociology, Post-modernity, and the "End of the Social"'. *Sociology*, 24: 3, 397–416.

Smart, B. (1992): *Modern Conditions, Postmodern Controversies*. London: Routledge.

Smart, B. (1999): *Facing Modernity*. London: Sage.

Sokal, A. and Bricmont, J. (1998): *Intellectual impostures*. London: Profile.

Starobinski, J. (1979): *Words Upon Words: The Anagrams of Ferdinand Saussure*. New Haven: Yale University Press.

Stearns, W. and Chaloupka, W. (eds) (1992): *Jean Baudrillard: The Disappearance of Art and Politics*. London: Macmillan.

Virilio, P. (1984): *L'Horizon négatif*. Paris: Galilee.

Virilio, P. (1986): *Speed and Politics*. New York: Semiotext(e).

Virilio, P. (1990): *Popular Defense and Ecological Struggles*. New York: Semiotext(e).

Virilio, P. (1991a): *The Aesthetics of Disappearance*. New York: Semiotext(e).

Virilio, P. (1991b): *L'Écran du desert*. Paris: Galilee.

Virilio, P. (1993): *L'Insécurité du territoire*. Paris: Galilee.

Virilio, P. (1994): *Bunker Archeology*. New York: Princeton University Press.

Virilio, P. (1996): *Cybermonde, La Politique du Pire*. Paris: Grasset.

Virilio, P. (1997): *Open Sky*. London: Verso.

Virilio, P. and Brausch, M. (1997): *Voyage d'hiver: Entretiens*. Paris: Parentheses.

Virilio, P. and Lotringer, S. (1997): *Pure War*. New York: Semiotext(e).

Wernick, A. (1984): 'Sign and Commodity: Aspects of the Cultural Dynamic of Advanced Capitalism'. *Canadian Journal of Political and Social Theory*, 8: 1–2, 17–34.

Zurbrugg, N. (1993): 'Baudrillard, Modernism and Postmodernism'. *Economy and Society*, 22: 4, 482–500.

Zurbrugg, N. (ed.) (1997): *Jean Baudrillard: Art and Artefact*. London: Sage.

Index